PENGUIN BOOKS

A Cockney Camera

Gordon Winter has worked as a journalist, author, publisher and broadcaster. He has been on the editorial staff of a number of weeklies, including *The Listener* and *Country Life*, on the board of the *Fortnightly* and other papers, and has held a number of senior posts in the BBC.

During the Second World War he served in North Africa, Italy and Greece. For many years he broadcast for the BBC in Italian, which he learnt during the campaign in Italy. After three years as Canadian representative of the BBC he returned to *Country Life* as Assistant Editor and then Chief Assistant Editor.

His other books include *A Country Camera*, a social history of rural life as shown in old photographs (this book is available in Penguins), and *The Golden Years*, a pictorial record of social life in the decade 1903–1913.

GORDON WINTER

A Cockney Camera

London's Social History

Recorded in Photographs

PENGUIN BOOKS

Penguin Books Ltd,
Harmondsworth, Middlesex, England
Penguin Books Australia Ltd,
Ringwood, Victoria, Australia
Penguin Books Canada Ltd,
41 Steelcase Road West, Markham, Ontario, Canada
Penguin Books (N.Z.) Ltd,
182–190 Wairau Road, Auckland 10, New Zealand

First published as *Past Positive* by Chatto & Windus 1971
Published as *A Cockney Camera* in Penguin Books 1975
Copyright © Gordon Winter, 1971

Printed in Great Britain by
Fletcher & Son Ltd, Norwich

Contents

Illustrations

Acknowledgements

I am grateful to Richard Church, and to William Heinemann Ltd., for permission to quote the passages on his childhood memories of bicycling from *Over the Bridge*.

I am indebted to the following for lending me the photographs in this book, and for their patience, kindness and courtesy in helping me with my research. Plates 1, 2, 9, 12, 23, 25, 28, 33, 41, 56, 67, 103, 111, 120, Victoria and Albert Museum. 3, 4, 5, 35, 39, 40, 42, 63, 69, 70, 114, 142, 154, 155, Birmingham City Library. 6, 8, 8a, 17, 32, 47, 85, 105, Chelsea Public Library. 7, 18, 26, 27, 46, 57, 58, 137, Lambeth Public Libraries. 10, Lady Page. 11, 44, 45, 148, 149, Kensington Public Library. 13, 14, 55, 64, 80, 86, 98, 99, 101, 104, 113, 147, Guildhall Library and Tonbridge Public Library. 59, 61, 62, 89, 90, 93, 94, Guildhall Library. 15, 16, 20, 21, 30, 31, 34, 68, 73, 74, Mrs Richard Moore. 19, Greater London Council Photograph Library. 22, 36, 37, 38, 48, 49, 115, 135, 150, Tower Hamlets Public Libraries. 24, 75, 76, 77, 78, 79, 117, 118, 129, 140, Miss Pat Higgs. 29, 71, 91, 92, 95, 96, 97, 130, 131, 136, 138, 151, Greenwich Public Libraries (a full set of Spurgeon prints will be found in *Grandfather's London* by O. J. Morris). 50, 72, 81, 100, 102, 116, 121, 122, 123, 124, 125, 126, 132, 141, D. C. Harrod (Olney Collection). 51, 52, 53, 54, 83, 134, Hampstead Public Library. 60, National Monuments Record. 65, 65a, Port of London Authority. 66, Bank of England. 82, 84, 87, 88, 106, 107, 109, 110, 127, 128, 139, 143, Peter Gerhold (Olney Collection). 108, E. E. Smith. 112, E. C. Robinson. 119, Museum of English Rural Life, Reading. 123, Miss S. G. Clarke. 144, 145, 146, Kodak Museum. 152, 153, Post Office Corporation.

Introduction

Any attempt at social history based on the evidence in old photographs tends to write itself. It is impossible to set out with preconceived ideas of what life was like in the Victorian–Edwardian era, and then produce a collection of photographs to illustrate those ideas; all one can do is to seek out the widest possible range of early photographs, choose the ones that seem interesting and relevant, and then present them in an order that will let them tell their own story. The result may prove as unexpected to the collector and caption-writer as it is to the reader of the book. When I had finished the task of gathering together the photographs on the following pages I was surprised to find that the quality of life that they recorded seemed noticeably less agreeable than that suggested by my earlier volume, *A Country Camera*.

In that book I tried to show what it was like to live in the English countryside between 1844 (roughly the beginning of negative–positive photography) and the outbreak of the First World War. That evidence had suggested—certainly to myself and I think to the average reader—that life in the country in the nineteenth century was frequently hard but seldom unpleasant. Men and women at the lower end of the social scale might find themselves overworked and underpaid, but the general condition of their existence was not usually such as to deprive them of human dignity and self-respect. The ultimate safeguard remained, as it had been for centuries, the self-contained and public nature of village life; little could happen without the whole community getting to know about it. If the squire oppressed Hodge, or Hodge's widow, or even oppressed them by the negative process of neglect, at least everyone in the neighbourhood would know and would be indignant. If the oppression was enough to offend accepted Church of England ethics, then the combined opinion of vicar and village, of priest and people, would be able to make itself felt.

The great difference between London and the English countryside during this same period was that in the capital the forces of public opinion were not effective in the same simple, direct way. In consequence, the life of those who sank into poverty, whether through fault or through misfortune, was not only hard but exceedingly unpleasant. The Victorians and Edwardians found themselves living, for the first time in human history, in a megalopolis without having as yet devised any effective way of coming to terms with the worst of its social consequences. Those who were comfortably off—the upper and middle classes—were not conscious that they were oppressing the poor; they simply did not know that the poor were being oppressed. Few of us appreciate how far our attitudes on questions of social justice have changed during the past 100 years. Opinions now held, as a matter of course, by those on the far right of today's political spectrum would have been considered radical and even revolutionary by our great-grandfathers. Views on the proper duty of the State to care for the aged and the sick and the helpless, accepted today as normal and middle-of-the-road, would have seemed outrageous or visionary to many of those portrayed in the following pages.

The contrasts between rich and poor in these photographs are the more striking if one remembers that, throughout the period when they were taken, London was the imperial capital of the largest and richest empire that the world had known. Prodigious wealth flowed in; yet somehow or other it flowed beyond the reach of a large proportion—perhaps the majority—of the capital's inhabitants. Judged solely by the evidence in these pages, I do not think that there can be any doubt that London in 1970 is a more agreeable city than it was in 1870—in spite of our having, in the mean time, suffered the economic disruption of two world wars and the disbandment of an empire.

London in the nineteenth century must have been messier, noisier, and dirtier than it is now; on the other hand, it was homelier, and more like a large, overgrown country town. Pockets of the countryside and of village streets continued to survive, except in the City and in Westminster and the West End. For the majority of Cockneys life was both less urban and less urbane. In fact the principal merit of London then, as compared with London now, must have been that it was smaller, and therefore easier to get out of.

There are, I know only too well, more gaps in this book than in its precursor; that was inevitable, if only because of the wider range of the capital's activities; many themes, such as the law, or the City, would provide ample scope for a similar book of their own. But some of the missing sections—for example, there is nothing on schools—owe their absence to my failure to find enough good pictures to justify their inclusion.

In searching for suitable photographs I have quarried in many museums and public libraries, in and out of London; and I am greatly indebted to the curators and librarians who have shown me so much courtesy and kindness and who have made their collections available at times to suit my convenience rather than theirs. But I have also been fortunate in being able to draw on some remarkable collections still in private hands; in this respect I am particularly grateful, both for their photographs and for their hospitality, to Mrs Richard Moore, Miss Pat Higgs, Mr Peter Gerhold and Mr D. C. Harrod. Finally, I would like to acknowledge my gratitude to Mr Robert McCartney, the Deputy Governor, for advice and information about photographs taken in the Tower of London, to Miss Janet Barber for her help with research, to Miss Anne Price for advising me on the dates of Victorian fashions, and to Miss Auriel Brown and to Mr Robin Masters and his colleagues of Photographic International for their skill in breathing new life into old and faded photographic prints.

1   The drawing-room at Broom House, Fulham, in the 1860s. The fortunate family who lived in this splendid Georgian house enjoyed the best of all possible worlds. They were only a carriage drive from St James's, but their peace and serenity were no more disturbed by the din of urban life than they would have been in the depths of Hampshire. Notice the slip-covers on all the chairs. The covers would have been left on during the family's normal use of the house and taken off only on grand occasions. The protection provided by them is one reason why so much good eighteenth-century furniture survives today. In the earlier years of the twentieth century it was often claimed that Victorians covered up the legs of their chairs and tables much as they covered up the legs of their women; legs were indecorous and could not be displayed. That is a myth; the purpose of the covers was essentially practical, and the provision of them on a generous scale had been made possible for the first time by the looms of Manchester.

Domestic Life

To enjoy life in London in the nineteenth century, the first and most important step was to choose the right parents. A man who was born into an upper- or middle-class home, or who inherited the ability to work his way into one, would find that life could be more rewarding than at any previous time in English history; for the urban poor, on the other hand, conditions were probably harder than they had been since the Wars of the Roses. Throughout these pages, therefore, the theme of Disraeli's *Sybil* keeps obtruding itself: England had become two nations—the rich and the poor. The photographs in this section point to the extremes of the social scale: to the rich or comfortably established, on the one hand, and the most wretched or the most recently arrived immigrants, on the other. Between them ran an infinite range of gradations that I have not attempted to show. The extremes tell their own tale.

2   The lawns of Broom House; July 1863. This is, of course, a posed photograph. The slow photographic plates of the period demanded that the subjects should keep still. But the posing itself tells us much. The photographer has seen his composition as a classical landscape with figures. Even the owners of the house have not been allowed to intrude into the foreground; and the gardener and under-gardener know their place, at a respectful distance from their employers. The scene sums up the long, golden afternoon of the Victorian era. Broom House was pulled down in 1912; the gardens, celebrated even in the early years of the twentieth century, and the wide lawns stretching down to the Thames, are now part of the grounds of Hurlingham Club. The house was the home of the Sulivan family, merchants and civil servants; one of them married the younger sister of Lord Palmerston, and the great man was a frequent visitor on Sundays.

3　The reigning family at Holland House. From the left, behind, are Mr Gray, an artist, Lady Muriel Fox-Strangways and the Earl of Ilchester. In front are Lady Bridport, the Dowager Lady Ilchester, and the Countess of Ilchester and her children. This study, of one of the ruling families of the British Empire, was photographed in July 1907, just at the moment when the power and wealth of the Empire had passed its peak. The matriarchal dowager has about her something of the prophetic air of Greek tragedy; we may fancy that she is peering into the distance, at the long years of decline that lay ahead.

4　A family party. All we know of this group is that it shows 'E. Chart Esquire and Others' and that Mr Chart was Clerk of the Works at Hampton Court Palace. I have included it because it was taken, in 1902, by Benjamin Stone, the photographer who took the preceding picture of the Ilchester family. The similarities between the two groups are striking. Yet the Ilchesters were among the greatest and most powerful in the land, and the Charts, though eminently respectable, occupied quite a modest niche in society. The middle classes of the day could afford to imitate very closely the manners and dress of the upper classes; indeed, to do so was the hallmark of respectability.

5   The Swanneries drawing-room at Holland
House, Kensington, in 1907. This room was a
nineteenth-century addition, in the Jacobean style of
the rest of the house. It has been furnished—most
of us would now say over-furnished—in the full
tide of Edwardian extravagance, so that for a
moment one wonders whether one is looking at a
drawing-room or an auctioneer's sale-room.
Holland House was the London home of the Earl
and Countess of Ilchester, and the name of the
room refers to the celebrated swannery, still
flourishing, at the family's Dorset seat at
Abbotsbury; notice the painting on the right and the
dead swan, presumably stuffed, hanging under it.
Matching patterns have been used for walls,
curtains and chairs—a practice recently revived.

6 The garden of Chelsea rectory; one aspect of the comforts of religion. The photograph is undated, but I would guess the early 1880s. The garden is carefully tended, though the lawns would not be thought much of by modern standards.

7 The Victorian upper middle class at home. This was not a rich man's house. It was the residence of Captain Brown, of West Side, Clapham Common, and Captain Brown and his family are seen on their lawn in the summer of 1888. The house, built about 1795, had previously been the home of John Gilliat, Member of Parliament for Clapham from 1834 to 1854.

8 (and 8a)   Lindsay House, Cheyne Walk, towards the end of the nineteenth century. Lindsay House, built in the late seventeenth century, when Chelsea was still a village some distance from London, had already been divided up into five separate houses when this photograph was taken, and the symmetry destroyed by individual alterations, but the original unity can be identified from the roof. Notice the jaunty back-view of the gentleman in the bowler hat. In the enlargement another figure, probably a woman, can just be made out behind him. My guess is that he is courting a servant girl from the house that is out of the picture on the right. She has come down to the gate to talk to him, and is hiding behind the wall out of sight of her mistress, because in that house, as in others of its day, admirers were not allowed in the kitchen. Advertisements for servants frequently included the warning: 'No followers.'

16

9 Tea in the garden. The photograph, though posed and taken as a joke, is a reminder that every middle-class London home, even the most modest, had at least one living-in servant. Many of them came from the large families of farm labourers' homes and graduated through the local farmhouse and the nearest country town before they reached the splendour of a situation in London. Richard Jefferies, in the 1870s, wrote of these young women: 'The girls are not nearly so tractable as formerly — they are fully aware of their own value and put it extremely high; a word is sufficient, and if not pleased they leave immediately. Wages rise yearly to about the limit of twelve pounds.' He meant £12 a year, not £12 a week. The fear that servants would leave seems to have haunted middle-class housewives. The novelist Saki summed it all up in his celebrated epigram: 'The cook was a good cook, as cooks go; and as cooks go she went.'

10   The servants of a successful London physician's household in the 'nineties. Seated in the front row are, from the left, the kitchen maid, the housemaid, the cook and the nurse. Standing behind them are the between-maid, the under-housemaid, the under-nurse and the coachman. At the back are the groom, the gardener, the butler and the footman. This photograph of the staff at Number 33, Cavendish Square, the London home of Dr Symes-Thompson, was lent to me by his daughter, Lady Page, who writes: 'My father had family prayers every morning and evening at nine a.m. and ten p.m., at which all the household attended. The staff sat in strict order of precedence on chairs ranged against the wall. The butler always came in last and shut the door. The nurse did not consider that she was one of the servants, and so sat apart. The whole of this group came with us to our country house in Oxfordshire during the holidays. The servants' hall in the basement at 33, Cavendish Square was, I used to think, the most comfortable room in the house. There was always a roaring fire and comfortable armchairs. I was welcomed there, but not in the enormous kitchen.

'A passage under the garden led to the stables. After riding in Hyde Park one could come back that way through the billiard room. There was a blow whistle and a speaking tube from the hall of the house to the stables, and I well remember that we had one of the first telephones in London. I had to stand on a chair to reach it. Patients who came to see my father left their golden guineas and golden sovereigns all over the place in his consulting room — they were too shy to give them to him. I had great fun at lunch-time conducting a sort of treasure hunt for the money.

'When someone came to the front door the footman would open the door, and then the butler would come forward to speak to the visitor or patient. In grander houses there were always two footmen — one of whom took the visitor's hat, stick and gloves.'

Nowadays, when domestic service has largely died out, the idea has grown up that there was a stigma attached to being a servant in a Victorian household. This is quite untrue. Domestic employment with a good family was much sought after; many of the Symes-Thompson servants stayed with the family all their working lives — two of them for over sixty years.

11 Home life at the other end of the social scale. A group of Irish settlers, probably from County Cork, in the yard of Market Court, off High Street, Kensington, about 1865. Before we look back with self-righteous indignation at the men and women struggling to maintain decency and self-respect in these pitiful surroundings, it might be as well to consider the living conditions of some of our own recent immigrants.

12   Fore Street, Lambeth, in the 1860s. The caged
bird on the wall on the right suggests an effort to
maintain the amenities of home life under difficult
conditions, though the bird's owner, looking out of
the window at the photographer, has almost
disappeared by movement during the long
exposure. Tell-tale marks below the windows, just
beyond the street lamp on the left, indicate the
survival of that very ancient urban practice—
throwing slops out of upper windows to save
carrying them downstairs.

13 Seven Dials: a slum of the 1890s. Disraeli in
Sybil refers to Seven Dials in the 1840s as a
disreputable neighbourhood where respectable
young women would be ill-advised to walk alone.
Sybil herself makes her way there at night, at great
personal risk, in an attempt to save her Chartist
father from arrest. Its reputation had changed little
by 1882, when W. S. Gilbert wrote ironically in
Iolanthe:

> *Hearts just as pure and fair*
> *May beat in Belgrave Square*
> *As in the lowly air*
>   *Of Seven Dials.*

21

14   After-care for prisoners in the 1870s. This remarkable picture, taken in 1877 or a little earlier, is not a photograph of an ordinary cheap dining-room. The figure on the left is a Mr Baylis, and he is standing outside his cook shop and lodging house in Drury Lane. After spending seven years in the police force, Baylis took over these premises in association with the Royal Society for the Aid of Discharged Prisoners, and provided a home and cheap food to men immediately after their release from prison. His work is recorded in *Street Life in London*, by J. Thomson and Adolphe Smith, who describe him as having acted as a guide to London's underworld for Charles Dickens and George Augustus Sala.

15 and 16   Victorian new women. Julia Smith (1799–1883), photographed in London in the early 1860s, was the youngest daughter of William Smith, Member of Paliament for Norwich and a leading supporter of the anti-slavery campaign. Julia was a keen advocate of women's rights and was active in the movements for higher education for women, married women's property rights and the early years of the campaign for women's suffrage. She was Florence Nightingale's aunt, and helped her in her post-Crimean work. Mrs Richard Moore, who lent me the photograph, writes: 'She was lively, amusing and vague. Once she stepped out of a second-floor window by mistake and landed on the lawn unhurt.' Perhaps her skirts acted as a parachute.

16   Madame Belloc (1830–1914). A photograph taken in London in the 1860s. Mrs Richard Moore writes: 'Madame Belloc was an exponent of Female Emancipation. She was a new woman of the 1850s. She toured Europe on foot with a girl companion, wearing rational dress, and was much stared at by the natives. She survived the siege of Paris, and became the mother of Hilaire Belloc and of Mary Belloc-Lowndes.'

17 A child's dream-world of the 1850s. This charming view of the garden of Cheyne House, Upper Cheyne Row, Chelsea, is almost certainly the earliest existing photograph of a rocking horse, and is also an early example of an attempt to obtain a panoramic view by joining two photographs together; the join is just to the right of the group of figures. The rocking horse has a little Windsor chair fitted at each end of the rocker for the use of younger brothers and sisters.

Children

Extreme contrasts between affluence and poverty are often more striking in early photographs of children than in those of adults, perhaps because the children were unaware of any condition of life other than their own. The urchins in Plate 18 lived in a world so remote from that of their near-contemporaries in Plate 17 that neither could have imagined the existence of the other. And yet, with one of those ironies by which fate redresses the economic balance, the children in the street probably suffered less from boredom than did the sheltered little creatures in the Cheyne Row garden. The latter must have led lives oppressively confined by the nannydom of du Maurier's 'Let's go and see what little Tommy is doing, and tell him he mustn't'. In their way the urchins may even have been healthier, because, if they survived at all, they acquired an early immunity to the diseases of dirt and squalor. Nowadays we are so accustomed to the clean and tidy streets of English cities, only mildly sullied by the excreta of the petrol engine, that we have forgotten that children who played in the streets in the nineteenth century played, inevitably, among the accumulated droppings of all the horses that had lately passed that way.

24

18 New Street, near Lambeth Dock, in the 1860s. Only a small minority of London children could play in the security of their own garden. For most of them the playground, throughout the nineteenth century, was the street outside their front-door. But this was no particular hardship; mum or your elder sister could sit on the doorstep and keep an eye on you, and there was never any need to be out of shouting range. Until the coming of the motor car, the kind of horse-drawn traffic that was encountered in residential streets seldom presented a hazard to young children.

19   Albury Street, Deptford, in 1911. Compare this street scene, with its typical atmosphere of a village community surviving in the East End of London, with Plate 18, photographed half a century earlier. The only important difference, from the child's point of view, is that the road as well as the pavement has been paved. The splendid carved wooden doorways, reminiscent of those still to be seen in Queen Anne's Gate, probably date from about 1700.

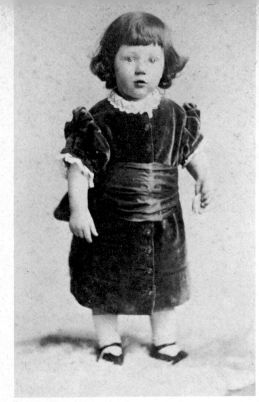

20 The age of lace, velvet and long hair. This little boy, photographed in a London studio in the early 1880s, is the son of the young woman on roller skates in Plate 34. His name was Ralph Wickham, he lived at Wimbledon and was the son of a London solicitor. Mrs Richard Moore, who lent me the photograph, writes: 'The Wickhams prided themselves on having their letters addressed to them simply at Wimbledon, without any street or number.'

21 An age when lace, velvet and long hair may have taken a little living down. The boy (he is a boy) almost certainly protested about being made to dress up as Little Lord Fauntleroy and prayed that none of his school friends would see the photograph. Frances Burnett's novel, about an ineffably refined American child who comes to England to inherit an earldom, had been a best-seller for 15 years when this portrait was taken, about the year 1900.

22 Meanwhile, in another part of the city . . . Children in a Poplar workhouse two or three years after Plate 21 was taken. During most of the nineteenth century an objective of the local authorities, in London as in the country, was to rid themselves of the burden of supporting pauper children. By 1908, when these infants were photographed, it was already widely recognised that the workhouse was in any case the wrong place to bring up children, but it was not until the middle of the twentieth century that the practice was finally abandoned.

23 A Little Dorrit of real life. This child, leading a blind beggar who is probably her father, was recorded by Paul Martin in a London livestock market some twenty years after the publication of Dickens's novel, but the scene of mutual wretchedness, shared between donkeys and humans, is one that he would have instantly recognised.

24 'I am the very model of a modern Major-General' or at least of one in the making. The little boy photographed in 1884, with his sisters Dorothy and Queenie, is Master Jack Scott; he grew up to be Major-General J. W. L. Scott, C.B., D.S.O., and at the time of his retirement was a deputy director of Medical Services in the Army. The father of the children, Dr Walter Scott, was for many years in general practice at Tulse Hill. Miss Pat Higgs, who lent me the photograph, writes: 'This doctor's family were by no means affluent and relied entirely, in those days before the National Health Service, on the ability of patients to pay their bills. Nevertheless, the family had a domestic staff of five: the childrens' nurse, a cook, a house-parlourmaid, a coachman and a boy. The boy's duty was to deliver medicines and clean the shoes. I have heard my mother say that the coachman kept his family on a wage of 30s. a week and that he was quite content with this.'

25 A pony before the days of the Pony Club. By 1913, when this was taken, the petrol engine was making itself felt in the streets of London, but it was safe enough for a child who was a competent horsewoman to ride unaccompanied. Before the First World War it was still a little advanced for a girl to ride astride.

26 and 27 A handsome line in hansom cabs. This child-size London cab would have been the envy of most children; to have it drawn by a goat instead of a pony was the last word in style, as the little girl clearly thinks. The model cab, in Brockwell Park, South London, can be compared with the real thing in Plate 131.

28 and 29   The water troughs in London streets in the 1890s were primarily intended for horses (see Plates 144 and 145); but they usually had a drinking fountain at one end, conveniently designed to be within reach of children. Nowadays the point of such street fountains is forgotten, and where they still exist they are hardly used. But in the nineteenth century it was by no means uncommon for poorer homes to have no water on tap, and certainly no drinking water. The barefooted little boy, photographed by Charles Spurgeon outside Greenwich Park on a bank holiday afternoon in 1884, is drinking sherbet, at a halfpenny a glass.

31

Dishes of the Day

It appears to be a peculiarity of the English moral outlook that each succeeding generation thinks it is the first to have discovered that sex is fun. Young men and women in the Naughty Nineties self-consciously believed that they were more venturesome and daring than their parents. Yet the Edwardians thought they had gone several steps farther, as did those just before them who considered themselves to be *fin de siècle*. The generation of the First World War were certain that the circumstances of their day caused them to be freer than the English had ever been before. And then there were those well-known decades of daring and rebellion against convention, the 'twenties and 'thirties ... until we arrived at the inevitable freedom of morals induced by the Second World War. And so it goes on.

But what of the 1860s and '70s? Surely that was the highpoint of mid-Victorian respectability and severity, when women obeyed implicitly the wishes of their parents or their husbands? The truth is, I suspect, that English women have been much the same, in the way they really behave as compared with the way they are supposed to behave, since Chaucer's Alisoun. Trollope's *The Prime Minister* was published in 1876, which we think of as a period of· female subjection and servitude; yet Mr Abel Wharton, Q.C., whose daughter wanted to marry a man he disapproved of, tells himself, and is told by his friends, that the days are long past when a father could stop his daughter from following her own wishes in such matters.

The young women in this section span the second half of the nineteenth century from the 1850s to the late 1890s. I have chosen them because they are all highly feminine and appealing. I doubt whether they were really very different, in their outlook on life, from their descendants of today.

30   Miss Hall; date uncertain, but probably 1859. A Paris fashion
plate of September of that year shows an almost identical row of
bows down the front of the dress and round the tops of the sleeves.
The severe hair-style could have been earlier; it had been worn by
Florence Nightingale many years before. But Miss Hall was surely a
beautiful girl by any standards. It would be interesting to know
whom she married, and what became of her.

31   *For manners are not idle, but the fruit*
                       Of loyal nature, and of noble mind.

We do not know what thoughts were in the mind of this young woman while she held the rather lengthy pose for her photograph, but she was probably familiar with Tennyson's Guinevere. The *Idylls of the King* were published in 1859, and this dress, with its full skirt and very full sleeves, would have been fashionable in 1861 or 1862. We know nothing of the girl except her name—Sylvia Hill.

32   The day of the crinoline. A private conversation by the Hans Sloane monument, outside Chelsea Old Church. The wearing of the crinoline, that is to say a full skirt supported by a bell-shaped petticoat held out by a series of wire hoops, reached the height of its popularity in the early 1860s. The girl on the left is a grown woman, so her feet are invisible. Her friend, or sister, wears the same crinolined skirt, but she is still young enough to be allowed the liberty of showing her ankles. The older girl is a good example of the contemporary A-line, running from narrow shoulders down to a broad base at the hem of the skirt.

33 What to wear on a summer afternoon in 1867. This young
woman was comfortably off; she has spent much time, and probably
not a little money, on making the best of her good looks, and gives
the impression that she is well pleased with the result. We do not
know her name, or that of her young admirer, but these are the gates
of Broom House, Fulham (see Plates 1 and 2). The young man's
stick, breeches and stockings seem more in keeping with a Scottish
hillside than the gardens of Broom House. Perhaps he felt that
Fulham was far enough from St James's for country wear to be
appropriate. I cannot make up my mind about the man on the right.
If he is the girl's father, then he seems strangely aloof. If he is there to
open the gate, then he is remarkably well dressed.

34   The height of elegance in the 1870s. The young woman is Dora Wickham, born a Halliday, and later the mother of young Ralph Wickham, seen in Plate 20. We know that the Wickhams had a high opinion of themselves—they liked their letters addressed to them simply as Mr or Mrs Wickham, Wimbledon—so we need have no doubt that on the occasion of this studio portrait Mrs Wickham was fashionably dressed. During the late 1860s full skirts had gradually begun to be drawn backwards. About 1870 the crinoline went out altogether and was replaced by the bustle, in which the skirt was supported by a small cage worn at the base of the spine. Though not particularly attractive in this example, it was among the most deliberately erotic of all fashions, pandering to every man's occasional wish that his dream woman should be steatopygous. Normally the skirt would have come right down to the ground, but here an inch or two of clearance is permissible because Mrs Wickham is dressed for roller-skating, a craze that was then the height of fashion.

35 A young woman of the Naughty Nineties. Mary C. French at the Tower of London on May 29th, 1898. Here is a fascinating example of the way in which women's fashions have come full circle. She could be a girl in a maxi-skirt in 1969 or '70, hair style and all. After many inquiries I have been unable to establish the identity of Mary French, or what she was doing at the Tower of London. A Mary Cassandra French, daughter of Hugh Mair, of Phyllis Court, Henley-on-Thames, was at that time the young wife of Major the Hon. Robert French; but Major French was in the Gloucesters, and I can find no record of the Gloucesters being stationed at the Tower on that date. Perhaps she was just visiting a friend.

Old Age

The existence of old-age pensions, and the security offered by the Welfare State, are now so much a part of our lives that it is difficult to realise how recently they were introduced. State social insurance, as such, began in Europe with Bismarck's sickness insurance bill of 1883; the first British social insurance legislation did not reach the Statute Book until 1911. Non-contributory old-age pensions began in Britain in 1908, under an Act that was largely the fruit of agitation by Sidney Webb and provided pensions for those over 70 who were needy and deserving. But state insurance for old-age pensions was not introduced in Britain until 1925. During the period with which this book is concerned, therefore, to be both old and poor was a fearful burden, the more so in London than in the country because of the anonymity and loneliness imposed by a great city. The shadow of the workhouse hung over the closing years of the poor, even though they themselves might escape its clutches.

36   A corner in the Hester Hawes alms-houses in Bow Lane, about 1912. There is nothing about this scene that suggests even an approach to comfort. There appear to be no curtains in the windows; the dustbin lid does not fit the dustbin; the grass between the flagstones is the result of neglect, not of design; and such attempts at gardening as can be discerned in the far corner are half-hearted. Compared with the conditions in the following photographs (Plates 37 and 38), however, it must have seemed bliss.

39

37 and 38   Poplar workhouse in 1905: the kitchen, and some of the inmates. The two photographs provide fascinating evidence of what that extinct institution, the workhouse, was like in its closing stages. The kitchens are well equipped, and the standards of cleanliness and care seem to be high, even allowing for the element of smartening up that is likely to have crept in on a day when everyone knew a photograph was going to be taken. The old women look well cared for and adequately fed; and the presence of pictures, plants and a parrot all suggest a reasonable attempt at providing a home-like atmosphere. But the room must have been very crowded for those whose only home it was, and all the faces that are not blurred by movement show signs of strain and anxiety, possibly caused, in part, by dislike of a photographic record being made to prove for all time one's sojourn in the workhouse. Three years after the photograph was taken, in 1908, came the introduction of a national scheme for a state old-age pension; state insurance against sickness and unemployment followed another three years later.

39 and 40 Saint Bartholomew's sixpenny charity, Saint Bartholomew's church-yard, 1902. Under the provision of this ancient Good Friday charity, twenty-one aged widows are each picking up a bun and sixpence from the tombstone of the donor of the charity. The point of the photographs lies in the faces of the widows. Many of them have the sunken mouths that betray toothless gums. In 1902, as it had been for countless centuries, this was a characteristic of the aged poor. There was no National Health Service to provide them with false teeth. It is a sharp reminder of the great leap forward in social conditions that we have made in this country within the past twenty-five years.

41 Mary Thompson in her 110th year. A photograph taken in London by W. R. Bailey on July 9th, 1863. In *A Country Camera* I included a photograph of Robert Morvinson, a carrier and shoemaker, taken in 1857. Robert Morvinson was 82 when the photograph was taken, and I pointed out that this meant that he was born in 1775, when the United States was still a British Colony. Mary Thompson beat Morvinson's record easily. She was born in Killesher, Co. Fermanagh on May 1st, 1754. A note that has survived with the photograph records that at the age of 110 she could read without glasses. The note continues: 'she is 100 years older than Lady Alice Cole, who, with Lady Jane Cole, is present in the picture, the fifth generation from that which saw the birth of Mary Thompson.' Lady Jane and Lady Alice Cole were daughters of the Earl of Inniskillen.

42 Lieutenant-General Sir Bryan Milman, K.C.B. This fine old gentleman, still looking every inch a soldier, was photographed in July 1898 at
the Tower of London, where he held the post of Resident Governor and
Major of the Tower. He was in fact appointed Major of the Tower—the
title given to the senior resident officer—in 1870, but the post was given
the additional title of Resident Governor, which it still carries, in 1874.
His rank was junior to that of the Constable, but the Constable does not
reside at the Tower.

Rural Survivals

The photographs of nineteenth-century London that are most commonly reproduced show busy scenes of horse-drawn traffic. From these it is easy to deduce, wrongly, that Victorian London consisted largely of streets thronged with cabs and carriages. The truth must have been very different. The crowded, bustling and highly urban area was small, and confined almost entirely to the City and the West End. Most of London still consisted of casual, totally unplanned surburban sprawl. Charles Dickens, whom we do not often think of as a town planner, complained in a letter to Miss Burdett-Coutts, 'If you go out into any common outskirts of the town now and see the advancing army of brick and mortar laying waste the country fields and shutting out the air, you cannot fail to be struck by the consideration that if large buildings had been erected for the working people instead of the absurd and expensive separate walnut shells in which they live, London would have been about a third of its present size.'

The debate about whether it would be better for London to build upwards or outwards still continues, unresolved, among architects and town planners. In his correspondence with Miss Burdett-Coutts, Dickens argued in favour of tall buildings—tower blocks as we would now call them—on the grounds that families living in a smaller London would have the pleasures of a country walk that much nearer to their front door, and also, less convincingly, that men would be able to live nearer to their work and 'would not have to dine at public houses'. He was, of course, totally disregarded, and the sprawl has continued ever since. But the disadvantages of living in a desert of bricks and mortar were greatly mitigated in Dickens's day because so many pockets of countryside survived within the urban mass. All over outer London former villages, in the process of being swallowed up by the tide of houses, retained something of their village character; and the green fields themselves were still, by today's standards, incredibly near.

43   Bishop's Walk, Lambeth. The date is uncertain, but I would guess about 1850, judging by the clothes and the general atmosphere. The lane led straight on to the river, as is clear from the notice: 'E. Searle, Boat Builder; Boats Let & Housed.' At about this time Searles also had a boat-house at Putney, near the start of the Boat Race. The whole of this area, with its pleasant riverside village atmosphere, was cleared to provide the site for St Thomas's Hospital.

44 and 45   The heart of bed-sitter-land a hundred years ago. Earls Court Farm as it was in the 1860s. Not long after these photographs were taken, Earls Court station was built on the site. Those who now live in the area can decide for themselves which version they prefer—the present or the past—and bear in mind that we are still swallowing up the English countryside at the same feckless rate. Earls Court Farm extended westward as far as the Kensington canal, which later became the West London Railway. In early Victorian times the village of Earls Court consisted of a few houses and cottages, mostly on the eastern side of Earls Court Road. On the western side of the road lay the farm and the Manor house. The librarian of Kensington Public Library, to whom I am indebted for this information, adds: 'North, south, east and west of the village lay open country, mainly farmland and orchards. The environs of the village, all within a half-mile walk, were: to the north, Edwardes Square and Pembroke Square; to the south, through Walnut Tree Walk, Little Chelsea; to the west the new West London cemetery and the Kensington canal; and to the east the village of Brompton. The lanes leading to these ran through fields or orchards.'

The barn in the two photographs is the same building, seen from a different angle, and can be identified by the clock with its hands missing. The flat, box-like structures in the foreground of Figure 45 are evidently cold frames. The tunnel construction behind them was probably designed to support netting over soft fruit—in this case, I would guess, strawberries.

46 Palace Yard, Ferry Street, Lambeth, in the 1860s. When the photograph was taken Palace Yard had already become dilapidated and down-at-heel, but it retained the compensation of a village atmosphere, and the freedom from traffic that enabled dogs to bask in the sun. In the first part of the nineteenth century there was comparatively little building south of the Thames, to the west of Lambeth Palace. This explains the otherwise puzzling reference by Wordsworth, in the sonnet *Composed Upon Westminster Bridge*, to London as 'All bright and glittering in the smokeless air'. The prevailing wind being from the south-west, there must have been many mornings when all the smoke had been blown away from that part of London that could have been seen by a watcher standing on Westminster Bridge.

47 Chelsea Old Church and Cheyne Walk in the 1860s. This can be compared with the picture of the two girls standing by the Sloane monument in Plate 32. Today's familiar complaint, that parish churches cannot afford to keep church clocks in working order, seems to have applied to the village of Chelsea in the 1860s. The clock says twenty minutes to ten; but judging by the position of the shadows, it must have been about noon.

48

48   London's East End in its cottage days. These two cottages were formerly on the East India Dock Road, east of the site of Poplar Hospital and facing the dock wall. The photograph was taken about 1860; the cottages were demolished in 1868. Both this picture and Plate 49 are poor photographs, but I have included them because they show London cottages with their own little cabbage-patches — an asset that more than compensated for the primitive and insanitary condition of the cottages themselves.

49   Lamb Gardens, Poplar, in 1870. Though the cottages may seem little more than hovels, their occupants had room to grow vegetables, and to have hutches, probably designed to house rabbits — kept for the table rather than as pets. These cottages, and those in Plate 48, were just the kind that were cleared away and replaced by the Peabody Buildings, with money provided by the American businessman and philanthropist, George Peabody. Peabody gave the then enormous sum of £500,000 expressly to build better housing for the working classes of London. For this, and for other generosity, he was offered a baronetcy by Queen Victoria, but declined it. Many of the Peabody Buildings still stand, and judged by modern eyes it is doubtful whether they provided accommodation that was an improvement on the cottages they replaced; but being many storeys high they certainly allowed, as Dickens proposed (see page 44), more Londoners to inhabit a given area.

50   Wandsworth High Street in the 1880s. Though this was a comparatively important suburban road in its day, the atmosphere of village peace persists. Most of the people in the picture are either walking or standing casually in the road without being in the least troubled by the traffic or the risk of being knocked down. Notice that the two women with umbrellas are using them as parasols.

51   The peace and quiet of Kilburn High Road. The corner of Eresby Road in about 1870. The district had already become sufficiently urbanised to have a gaslit street lamp, and the name of the road on a post at the corner, but the little Georgian houses date from the time when Kilburn was quite a remote village, and the country atmosphere persists. The notice to the left of the tree behind the man in the white apron announces that C. Crook, Job and Post Master, has broughams and carriages to let. (See also Plate 126.)

50

52 In the heart of the country, near Swiss Cottage. The date is not known, though I would guess somewhere round the turn of the century; the print comes from Hampstead Public Library and is described simply as being taken at the site of Avenue Road. It is a reminder of the ease with which the Londoner, even seventy years ago, could escape into the countryside on a Saturday afternoon.

53 Flask Walk, Hampstead, in about 1910. Although this photograph was taken about forty years after Plate 51, Hampstead had managed then, as it has since, to retain much of its village atmosphere, whereas Kilburn High Road has become a torrent of traffic roaring between embankments of concrete and glass.

54   Gipsies in a field at Fortune Green, West Hampstead, in 1887. The use of semi-tubular tents, to supplement the accommodation in their caravans, was common among English gipsies in the nineteenth century. In terms of horse transport, and the size of London, Fortune Green must have seemed about as far from the capital in the 1880s as St Albans would be today.

55   Gipsies on a plot of vacant land in Battersea in the 1870s. Unlike the gipsies in Plate 54, this family are not camping on the outskirts of London, but have established a way of life within the capital itself. J. Thomson, who claimed to know the family, recorded that the owner of the caravan was William Hampton and that the woman sitting on the steps, Mary Pradd, was murdered a few weeks after the photograph was taken.

52

56 A soap warehouse at Fore Street, Lambeth, in 1868. The Thames was London's main commercial artery, as it had been for centuries. Yet here was a Thames-side warehouse conducting its business at a pace that one might have supposed to be more appropriate to a sleepy market town. The soap was no doubt brought to the warehouse by barge. Now it is being unloaded, possibly into the cart in the background, using only the workman's muscles and a mechanical device unchanged since the Middle Ages.

The Day's Work

I have made no attempt in these pages to provide a pictorial record of London at work in Victorian and Edwardian days. I have not tried to do so partly because comparatively few photographs were taken, inside factories, warehouses and offices, which actually depict work in progress; such photographs as survive usually show the buildings or plant empty or static—a limitation imposed by the difficulty of making rapid exposures in an indoor light. Moreover, in the nineteenth century London was not primarily an industrial city; it was a great seaport, the seat of government and the centre of the Empire's finance and commerce. To a large extent, therefore, Londoners escaped the factory conditions that defaced the industrial regions of Britain during the period. Much of the work done in London still depended to a remarkable extent on manual operations. After all, it is only today that automation has begun to catch up with the processes, for example, of banking. The photographs in this section have been chosen partly because they show how much London still depended on man-power and muscle-power, and partly because they suggest— and I suspect that this was the case—that much of London's work went on at an almost rural pace. The impetus and inhuman rhythm of mechanisation was a characteristic of Manchester and the industrial North; London, until 1914, somehow managed to remain opulent and powerful without it.

57 and 58   The pulsating heart of Empire in the 1860s. Hunt's Bone Works, in Fore Street, Lambeth; Mr. Hunt himself is standing at his office door. There is no direct evidence that these photographs were taken by the same photographer at the same time as Plate 56, and they have reached me from different sources, but it is a reasonable guess that they were. When we are told that Britain's industrial and commercial methods are out of date it may be some compensation to reflect that

perhaps some of them always have been. In point of fact, all the buildings in the Fore Street area were pulled down not long after these photographs were taken. They met their fate not because they were inefficient, and were swept away by the free play of market forces and the coming of more modern methods of production, as one might suppose. They were pulled down because the bone factory offended the noses of Members of Parliament at Westminster on the opposite side of the river.

59   Paviours ramming granite pitching at the east end of Holborn Viaduct; September 14th, 1869. This must have been hard physical work, and it was evidently a fine day. Yet every workman in the picture is wearing a hat. The only explanation that I can think of is the nineteenth-century belief that warm sun could be dangerous if it fell direct on a man's head.

   Richard Jefferies had a poor opinion of the London navvy. In the 1870s he paid one of his rare visits to the capital, and described a road gang at work. 'Recently I had occasion to pass through a busy London street in the West-End where the macadam of the roadway was being picked up by some score of men, and, being full of the subject of labour, I watched the process. Using the right hand as a fulcrum and keeping it stationary, each navvy slowly lifted his pick with the left halfway up, about on a level with his waistcoat, when the point of the pick was barely two feet above the ground. He then let it fall—simply by its own weight—producing a tiny indentation such as might be caused by the kick of one's heel. It required about three such strokes, if they could be called strokes, to detach one single small stone. After that exhausting labour the man stood at ease for a few minutes so that there were often three or four at once staring about them, while several others lounged against the wooden railing placed to keep vehicles back.' *Plus ça change* . . .

60 Constructional work in progress at Holborn Viaduct, 1869. When we look back at some of the magnificent engineering achievements of a century ago it is sobering to reflect that this is how many of them were carried out. I suspect that the photograph sums up the mid-Victorian attitude to constructional work: the muscles of men, using a device of the most primitive and elementary kind, alongside the new and not yet fully exploited power of steam. The left-hand half of this photograph could have been Elizabethan; only the right-hand half suggests the drive behind the Victorian age.

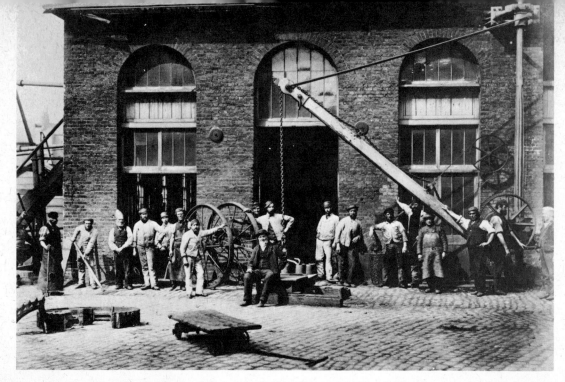

61 Employees at the distillery of Octavius Smith, Grosvenor Road, Pimlico, about 1870. Several of the men are posing ostentatiously with the implements of their work, which once again are a reminder of how much reliance was still being placed on muscle in small or medium-sized industrial firms of the period. The derrick, however, which is controlled by the manually operated gear-wheels on the right, appears to have a power-take-off running out just below the roof above the right-hand window, and transferred downward through the vertical shaft. Hats worn at work seem to have been obligatory at that time (compare Plate 59, and indeed all the other pictures in this section). This may have been no more than a matter of convention, or may have had the practical intention of keeping the hair clean. Evidently Andy Capp's irremovable headgear has a long tradition behind it.

62 *Rus in urbe* in the Grosvenor Road. All we know about this charming photograph is the description: 'An employee at the distillery firm of Octavius Smith.' Though growing grapes might perhaps be considered part of the process of a distillery, I doubt whether Octavius Smith made brandy. The grapes were no doubt intended for the table of Mrs Octavius Smith; and the gardener, then as now, was more conveniently carried on the books of the distillery than on Mr Smith's private account. Perhaps our industrial habits have not entirely changed. Not long ago a firm of efficiency consultants, making a tour of an English factory, were repeatedly barred from entry into one small building, on the grounds, they presumed, of industrial secrecy. When they finally got inside they found that it was being used for growing tomatoes.

58

63 In the days when the pound in your pocket was really not devalued; workmen pouring gold into moulds at the Royal Mint, Tower Hill, in March 1898. There is something so enduringly English about this photograph that I feel it could have been taken yesterday, were it not that the metal being poured is gold and not cupro-nickel, and that there is not a half-empty mug of cold tea anywhere to be seen.

64   A London sign-writer of the 1870s. We do not know this man's name, presumably because he asked the photographer to preserve his anonymity, but we know a surprising amount about him. He was a Parisian by birth, and began his working life as a linen draper's assistant before coming to London via Chicago and New York. His earnings as a sign-writer were low—between ten and fifteen shillings a week, a meagre income even in the 1870s. He was, however, befriended by the novelist, George Moore, who bought him a suit of clothes and set him up in a furnished room where he was better able to work. At the time when the photograph was taken the man's ambition was that by dint of frugal living he might save enough to return to France and buy a small shop. We have a record of his diet during this period: breakfast, cocoa and bread and butter; dinner, a pennyworth of potatoes with a herring or haddock and a cup of tea; supper, two pennyworth of bread and cheese. He spent nothing on drink. It remains a puzzle that a man of industry and sobriety, and not without ability, should have found it so difficult to make a decent living amid the prosperity of Victorian London.

65 and 65a   Workmen shovelling Thames mud out of a dredger at Crossness. At this time the docks of the East and West India Docks Company at Blackwall and the Isle of Dogs had to be dredged frequently for the removal of accumulated silt. In the mid-nineteenth century the silt was unloaded from barges and placed behind the river walls surrounding the Isle of Dogs, a very low-lying area. When that site was filled the docks company bought 100 acres of marshland at Crossness, and built barge-pens, machinery and mud-chutes, so arranged that the barges could be emptied by means of land dredgers and the silt distributed over the marshes. But the buckets of the land dredgers were not able to pick up the mud from the bottom of the barges, and this job had to be done by hand. Bearing in mind that the Thames was London's principal sewer, it must have been one of the least agreeable ways of earning a living, even in industrial England in the nineteenth century.

61

66   The Consols office, the Bank of England, 1894. If it were
possible to photograph security as the Victorians understood it this
would be the picture. An adequate income from Consols (short for
Consolidated Annuities and meaning Government securities) was the
ambition of every Victorian who aspired to financial independence.
The state of Consols provided the kind of index to the well being of
the moneyed classes that Mother Carey's stall provided for the poor
(see page 80). Disraeli himself, in *Vivian Grey*, remarked: 'There is
nothing like a fall in Consols to bring the blood of our good people of
England into cool order.' Employment in the Consols office must
also have represented the acme of security to the young men
observed rather languidly at work in it.

67　The lawn outside Lambeth Palace library in the 1860s. No information has come down to us with the photograph, beyond its self-evident impression of peace and security in the heart of London. The boy is about 14; the woman, from her apron, is probably a domestic, perhaps a nurse; the caged bird has been taken into the garden for an airing. No one seems to have minded a thick growth of daisies on the arch-episcopal lawn.

The Church

In London, as in all other great cities, the impact of the Church in the nineteenth century on people's daily lives was much less than in the villages. But judged by today's standards it was immensely strong and vigorous, and still provided a haven of eighteenth-century calm for those whose profession it was. Church-going, among Londoners, was more an accepted social practice than it is now; that is to say, people still went to church because it was expected of them — though perhaps not as much as we are inclined to suppose. Trollope, in *The Prime Minister*, published in 1876, gives an account of a conversation between the elderly QC, Mr Abel Wharton, and his sister-in-law about Mr Lopez, a suitor to his daughter's hand whom Mr Wharton considers undesirable. When Mr Wharton complains that nothing is known of Lopez's religious background, his sister-in-law replies tartly: 'He goes to church, just as you do — that is, if he goes anywhere; which I daresay he does about as often as yourself, Mr Wharton.'

68   A bishop in the making—Winfrid Burrows in 1862, at the age of four. Winfrid's mother, Maria Burrows, was the wife of a London clergyman, so their clothes can be taken as examples of what vicarage wives and children wore in London on smart occasions. Winfrid grew up to be a credit to his parents, and became Bishop of Truro and later Bishop of Chichester.

69   The Dean of Westminster at the turn of the century. The Very Rev. J. Armitage Robinson with (*left*) Mr W. R. Lethaby, the Abbey architect, and Dr Edward Scott. I have chosen this photograph of the Dean not only because he was a distinguished person of his period but also because he is such a notable example of the truth that men develop faces, as well as manners, to fit the age in which they live. To modern eyes he looks as though he has stepped straight off the stage of an Oscar Wilde comedy; in fact, *The Importance of Being Ernest* had made its first West End appearance shortly before this photograph was taken. Notice, incidentally, the beautifully polished boots. Most men in the nineteenth century do not seem to have been greatly concerned about the gleam of their footwear, and I have always supposed that the importance of shiny toe-caps did not become generally accepted until the First World War, but this does not seem to have applied in the precinct of Westminster.

70   Plain-clothes policemen employed at Westminster Abbey in 1897. Even at a distance of seventy years, no one would have been likely to mistake these stalwart figures for vergers, or for casual members of the public looking round the Abbey. They may in fact have been employed specially in connection with Queen Victoria's Diamond Jubilee. But if their presence in the Abbey implied that the public were free to wander at will through the building, and that the plain-clothes men were there to keep an eye on things, then there had been a marked change in policy during the century. In the 1840s Disraeli complained that one of his characters, Egremont, on his first visit to the Abbey, 'beheld the boards and spikes with which he seemed to be environed, as if the Abbey were in a state of siege; iron gates shutting him out from the solemn nave and the shadowy aisles; scarcely a glimpse to be caught of a single window; while on a dirty form some noisy vergers sat like ticket porters'. Disraeli added, for good measure: 'There is not perhaps another metropolitan population in the world that would tolerate such conduct as is pursued to "that great lubber, the public" by the Dean and Chapter of Westminster, and submit in silence to be shut out from the only building in the two cities which is worthy of the name of a cathedral. But the British public will bear anything; they are so busy speculating in railroad shares.'

71   A tea-stall run by the Church of England Temperance Society
in 1885. Drunkenness was a much more serious social evil then than
it is now (when we count our blessings we seldom remember that the
present must be one of the soberest ages in the whole of English
history), and a primary object of such mobile tea-stalls was to ensure
that the working man did not spend his money on strong drink
simply because no alternative was available.

72 The Church triumphant: a Sunday-school procession in Wandsworth High Street around the turn of the century. This enthusiastic mixture of Anglicanism, patriotism and general jollity would surely bring a gasp of wonder at the size of the crowd from any modern London vicarage. I cannot make out what exactly was going on on this particular occasion. The band is in full blast and the young ladies on the platform are in full giggle, but no one seems to be making a speech, and the procession itself has come to a halt. Whatever is being sorted out or moved on by the mounted policeman and his companion on foot, it is nothing very serious. Here, incidentally, is a remarkable example of the absolute importance, in those days, of wearing a hat. I have examined the whole of this crowd with a magnifying glass and cannot find a man, woman or child with a bare head.

Medicine

One of the effects of the National Health Service is that it has levelled out the earnings of London doctors. In the nineteenth century a London doctor whose practice was successful, even if it was not fashionable, was distinctly rich by today's standards, though he might not have thought himself so by his own. A fair fee was a golden guinea—worth more than ten times as much as 21s. today. On the other hand, doctors who worked among the poor, as a great many did from a sense of vocation, were much worse off than they are today under the Health Service. They could only earn what their patients could afford to pay, and only too often that was nothing at all. Some people joined medical insurance clubs at a small weekly subscription, but it was not until 1911 that Lloyd George's National Health Insurance Act introduced the panel-patient system, with some degree of assured income for the doctors concerned; and even that was opposed at the time, on the grounds that it would interfere with the doctor–patient relationship.

The great London hospitals were run, of course, entirely without financial support from the State. In many ways it is remarkable how little these hospitals have changed in the past 100 years, as is clear from the following brief account of the out-patients' department at St Bartholomew's Hospital written by a 22-year-old doctor, Norman Moore, in a letter to his mother dated June 2nd, 1869:

'I sit on a chair in a little room and hold a pen, a little board and a quantity of square bits of paper. Before me is a box with a slit in the top. Outside is a horde of patients. On Tuesday there were 270. I beckon to one and he comes in, having been given a tin ticket by the porter. He puts the ticket into the box with the slit. I ask his name and write it, the date and my own name on a bit of paper on my small board. I then ask him what is the matter and how long he has been ill, how much he drinks a day, and if he has been in the hospital before, and make my own observations on his symptoms.

'I then diagnose his disease: if it seems bad, or a chronic case, I give him an out-patient's letter and send him over to the Assistant Physician. If it seems slight, or an occasional attack, I write a prescription for the patient and tell him when to call again. He takes my prescription over to the dispensary and receives the medicine at once. If I cannot make out a case I consult Mr Jukes, a House Physician. He is receiving patients at the same time. As far as my experience goes, three pints of beer a day is the average quantity drunk by an English workman.'

When he wrote this letter young Dr Moore's qualifications were a degree in natural science at Cambridge, and six months' residence at Bart's. The service that Bart's offered was entirely free. He wrote to his mother: 'All you have to do to be admitted to Bart's is to be ill, and to be poor.'

73 Dr Norman Moore (later Sir Norman Moore, Bt., President of the Royal College of Physicians) at his fireside at 94 Gloucester Place in the year 1900. This is the Dr Moore whose letter to his mother, written when he was a very young doctor, is quoted above. At that time he assured his mother that he could live comfortably in London on £100 a year. When the photograph was taken he was a successful figure in his profession, as Assistant Physician at Bart's, and was earning about £1,000 a year. Some indication of the purchasing power of that income is given by the knowledge that his family engaged a new cook in December, 1891; her wages were £24 a year.

Mrs Richard Moore, to whom I am indebted for this photograph, writes: 'Dr Moore is wearing, as he had for the previous 20 years, and would for the next 20, a frock coat, a shirt with a wide turned-down collar tied with a loosely knotted broad silk tie. Here he is in his slippers, but for work he wore lace-up boots, and a tall hat in which he kept his stethoscope, which was a narrow wooden tube like a pea-shooter, about nine inches long. Dr Moore was particularly attached to "a good fire" and it is interesting to see that he has a wood fire in the photograph, although he is in the middle of London.'

Dr Moore's son, Sir Alan Moore, has recorded of him: 'He believed in keeping warm. Long drawers with the socks overlapping were considered essential. Draughts he thought dangerous. If he caught sight of an open window the order to shut it became almost a reflex. Out-of-doors he would face any weather, but indoors—warmth above all things.'

Mrs Moore tells me that when the family moved into Gloucester Place in 1891 the rent was £300 a year. The road was made up, but still had a stony surface, muddy in winter. Dr Moore's son Alan, when a small boy, thought that the Cromwell Road was called the Crumble Road, and that it was so called because of its rough surface. 'It was muddy after rain,' he writes, 'but there were crossing sweepers. Traffic was not heavy. Generally, looking down the street, a hansom cab was to be seen, within range of the whistle that everyone kept in the hall. There was a code of whistles, to indicate whether you were calling a hansom or a four-wheeler.'

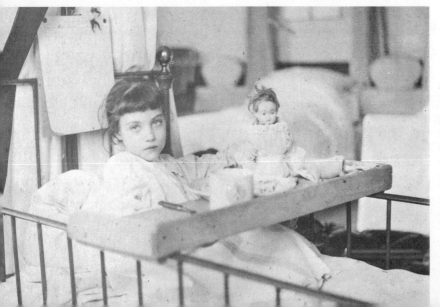

74 Florrie, a patient at Bart's in September, 1885. We have no record of what was wrong with her, though she must have been one of Norman Moore's patients. The photograph bears its own witness to how well she was cared for.

69

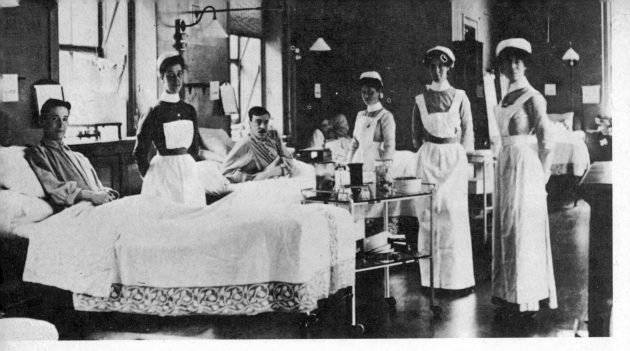

75   Belgrave Ward, St George's Hospital, in 1908. Miss Pat Higgs, who has kindly lent me this and the following photographs of St George's Hospital, writes: 'Although there was no motor traffic outside the hospital at the time, there was a great deal of noise. The horse buses stopped just outside the hospital (see Plate 140), and their conductors were incessantly calling out their destinations. On one occasion, when a physician was asking a student what he could hear in a patient's chest with the stethoscope, the student answered: "All I can hear, sir, is: 'ammersmith, 'ammersmith".' Miss Higgs points out the 'appalling unsmartness' of the two nurses on the right who must, she suggests, have been 'the newest of probationers'.

76   Grosvenor Ward, St George's, in 1903. The circular indicator on the wall was the equivalent of the present 'bleep' call system. It was operated by a porter in the main hall, and the pointer clicked round to 'accident', 'visitors out', 'chapel', 'house physician' or the names of individual consultants.

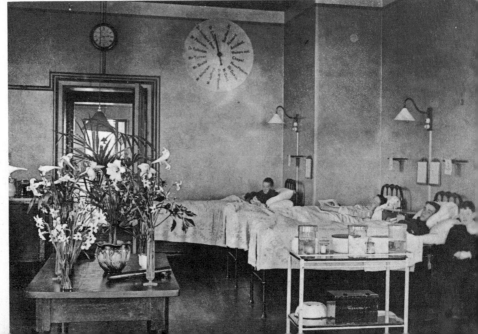

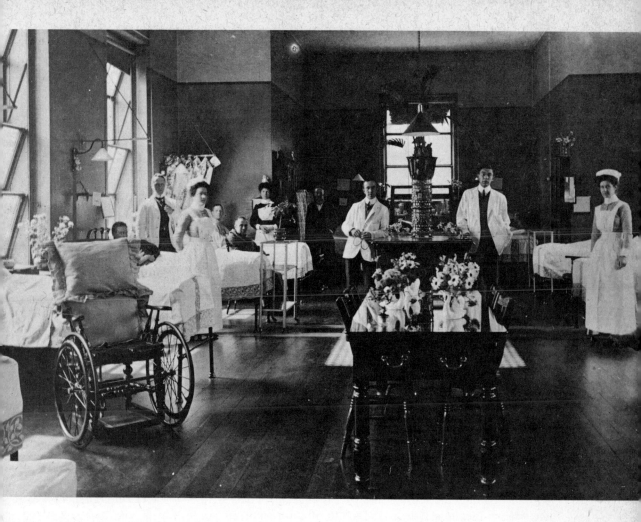

77 Williams Ward, St George's Hospital, in 1909. Miss Higgs
points out how little the hospital wheel-chair has developed in the
past sixty years, though in those more leisured days the pillows were
frilled. She writes: 'The floors were not washed, but a certain amount
of hygiene was maintained by the annual visit of an army of Italian
workmen who scraped off the polished surface, and with it the dirt
and germs, ready for a fresh application of polish. The shape of the
nurses' caps appears to have gone full circle. In the 1920s and later,
the cap covered the hair with a hard line round the forehead. Now the
cap is again made up as small as possible, and perches on top of the
hair in the style of the sister in the left background who, with the
length of her skirt hidden, could be a sister of today in every respect.'

71

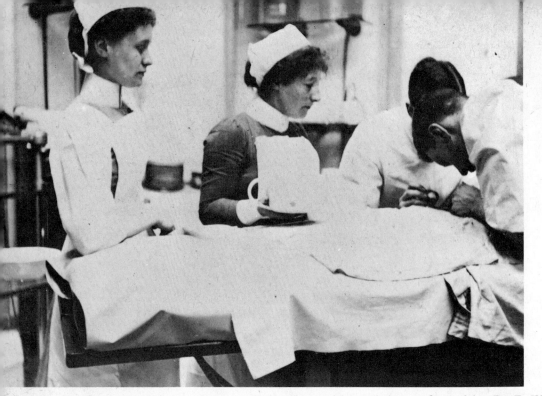

78 A minor operation—probably circumcision—being performed by Dr F. W. Higgs in the West Theatre, St George's Hospital, in 1905. Note that no masks or rubber gloves are being worn, though Nurse Exley, on the left, appears to be wearing protective sleeves. Nurse Exley was born in 1879, so she was 26 when the photograph was taken. She later married, and her daughter, Mrs Makepeace, writes: 'I had always understood that the nurses' hair had to be tucked into their caps, but that doesn't seem to be the case here. Perhaps some sisters were stricter than others. Mother had rather pretty hair, I believe, and liked to show it. In those days nurses had to work long hours with very short off-duty times. Weekends were few and night duty went on for weeks or even months at a time. Mother used to say she was afraid to sit down on night duty for fear of going to sleep.'

79 Nurse Exley and Dr F. W. Higgs in the West Theatre, St George's Hospital, 1905. Dr Higgs was 24 at the time. Nurse Exley was a little older; the London hospitals in those days insisted on a minimum age of 23 at the beginning of a nurse's training. Today they begin at 18, and a nurse can be fully trained and a ward sister before the age of 23, when her grandmother was considered only just mature enough to embark on a career.

72

80   Medical practice at the unqualified end of the profession. This pedlar, in a London back street in the 1870s, offers 'Our new cough preventative' at $\frac{1}{2}d$. and $1d$. a packet, seven packets for $6d$., on the grounds that 'prevention is better than cure'. He also advertises 'Peppermints, same price', Moore's Herbal Pills and cough lozenges. His clean stiff collar and noticeably well-groomed appearance are no doubt part of the professional manner on which his trade depends, but he must have done well or he would not have been able to afford such clothes. Quack pedlars worked on the principle: 'If it don't lengthen the life of the buyer it lengthens the life of the seller.' Their success depended almost entirely on the skill of their patter.

Shops and Markets

Feeding the people of a city as large as London towards the end of the 19th century was in many ways a more remarkable achievement than it is today. Distribution from the rail depots was entirely horse-drawn, as was all public and private transport, and this meant that London had an enormous population of horses which also had to be fed. Though refrigerated meat had begun to be imported in the 1880s, the supply of fresh milk in London remained a problem, and was still being solved in many parts of the city by the ancient practice of keeping stall-fed cows in sheds in which they spent practically the whole of their lives. In the suburbs it was easier; dairy farmers often managed to retain at least one or two fields within otherwise built-up areas.

81 Putney High Street in 1881. This butcher's shop, which served the more prosperous section of the population of Putney, seems to be uncertain about its name. T. B. Pook is plain for all to see over the open, unglazed shop front, but the tricycle and the smart little delivery cart are both labelled Harriott, Butcher, High Street, Putney. The butcher evidently lived over the shop, and the butcher's wife took pride in her lace curtains. Unlike today's shops, this one retained a parlour and a window on the ground floor; but notice the iron rod running just above the window to the post at the side; it was designed for the display of meat hanging on hooks when the shop-front itself was overcrowded.

82 Another Putney butcher of the same period; this one evidently served less prosperous customers. S. W. Lydiat describes himself as 'Pork Butcher and Dairyman'. He is probably the man in the dark overalls outside the dairy half of the shop, which also sells bread and eggs. His wife, in the butcher's apron, appears to have taken on the tougher job of cutting and serving the meat.

83   A shopping expedition at the turn of the century in England's Lane, Haverstock Hill, Hampstead. The butter in Raworth's window is priced at a 1s. up to 1s. 4d. a pound. That was 70 years ago, so it is a remarkable reminder of the way in which food prices have been kept down in Britain since that date, compared with the price of everything else. The two young women wheeling the perambulators appear to be discussing something much more exciting than the price of butter.

84 The little men round the corner. When this photograph was taken at Wandsworth (the river in the foreground is the Wandle) London suburbs abounded in small tradesmen. Do-it-yourself was almost unheard of. Competition was intense. P. Whitby, Gas, Bath & Hot Water Fitter and Plumber & General House Decorator, proclaims that he does Sanitary Work On Most Modern Principles. Next door to him is T. Davis, Builder & Decorator. Perhaps the latter found that there was not enough work for both of them, for he is a newsagent as well. Further down the row are a shop that proclaims Glass Cut and Windows Repaired; and finally C. Timson, Licensed Chimney Cleaner & Carpet Beater.

85 A saddler's shop at 312 King's Road, Chelsea. In the days of horse transport, craftsmen-saddlers flourished in all the London suburbs. A clue to the date of the photograph is provided by the placard advertising one-guinea season tickets for Saturday concerts at the Crystal Palace, beginning on Saturday October 10th. Paxton's Crystal Palace, originally designed for the Great Exhibition of 1851, was moved to Sydenham in 1854. October 10th fell on a Saturday in 1857, 1863, 1868 and 1874. My guess would be 1868.

86   A second-hand furniture dealer at the corner of Church Lane, Holborn, in 1877. From what one can make out, most of his wares seem to have hovered on the narrow border between second-hand furniture and junk, but the pair of rush-seated chairs are in good condition. When the photograph was taken they would have changed hands for a shilling or so; it would be interesting to conjecture what they would fetch now. I cannot make up my mind whether the young woman on the right is holding a bottle, wrapped in newspaper for the sake of respectability, or a vase that she has just bought from the dealer.

87 The last herd of cows in Putney; Morrison's dairy in about 1905. The cows must have been part of a much larger herd. Even in the days of cheap and plentiful labour, two cowmen would not have looked after six cows. The figure on the left in the wing collar is possibly Mr Morrison himself.

88 Mr Morrison's transport fleet: a dairyman's cart; seven three-wheeled hand-carts; and at the far end, a milk float. F. I. Morrison, of Springfield Farm Dairies, had two other shops in Putney. He proclaimed with pride on all his shop fronts that the firm was established in 1776. He also advertised: 'Absolutely pure milk from our own cows; Alderney cows kept for infants and invalids.' Milk retailers who did not have their own herds usually bought from farms near London by contract. Writing in 1879, Richard Jefferies describes an arrangement made with a leading metropolitan dairy company. 'The farmer is asked to fix a minimum quantity which he will engage to supply daily, but he can send as much more as he likes. This permits of economical and natural management in a dairy.' Jefferies records the price received in summer as about 5d. or 5$\frac{1}{2}d$. per imperial gallon, which would then be retailed in London at about 1s. 8d. a gallon. The price, he considered, gave the farmer almost no profit. Here, however, is yet another example of the cheapness of food in London in our time, when milk costs 1s. a pint, compared with 2$\frac{1}{2}d$. in 1879. The purchasing power of money has changed by very much more than that in ninety years.

89 Covent Garden Market in about 1890. The drum-shaped circular baskets, seen in the foreground and on two of the carts, were traditional to Covent Garden, and have only recently disappeared. Porters carried them balanced in tall columns on their heads, and took pride in the number they could carry. Circular baskets and barrels continued in use for so many centuries because, I suppose, their shape gave them strength. The amount of wasted space on a waggon or in the hold of a ship is otherwise inexplicable.

90 Whitechapel hay and straw market in April 1899. At one time the principal market to provide fodder for London's horses was in the West End street that we still call the Haymarket. That market was moved out to Regent's Park in 1836, however, and the principal fodder market then became the haymarket in Whitechapel High Street. Most of the hay came in from the surrounding countryside on carts, as seen here. But some came up the Thames by barge and some, from farther afield, by rail. The merchants normally went out and bought the hay in the stack, or standing in the meadow. Richard Jefferies, in 1879, refers to standing grass crops having been sold a few years previously for £5 the acre. 'This year,' he adds, 'auctions of standing grass crops hardly realised 30s. an acre.'

91 The top end of the street-trader market; a shrimp stall in Greenwich, 1884. This little business, recorded by the great photographer of London street characters, Charles Spurgeon, must have been exceptionally prosperous to support three salesmen, probably a father and two sons. The whole scene has an air of prosperity. The poster on the left advertises dinners at 1*s*. 6*d*. and York ham at 9*d*. These were substantial prices. The shrimps were probably a penny a bag.

Standing on One's Own Feet

In an age when the State had not yet decided that it was supposed to be benevolent, and when poverty tended to be regarded — by those who did not suffer from it — as a fault rather than as a misfortune, the Victorians laid stress on the virtue of standing on one's own feet. For the small traders who thronged the streets of nineteenth-century London, this phrase had a particularly harsh significance: they stood in the roads on their own feet because they had not enough capital to carry on their business in any other way. Even within the street-traders, there was a hierarchy. Those at the bottom sold only what they could carry on their persons; those at the top had small stalls and a recognised pitch.

The prosperity of the little traders was a good guide to the prosperity of the poor, who were their customers. Disraeli, in *Sybil*, makes this point well, in a conversation between discontented workers who are thinking of going on strike.

'"I am all for a strike," said Mick.

'"'Tisn't ripe," said Devilsdust.

"But that's what you always say, Dusty," said Mick.

"I watch events," said Devilsdust. "If you want to be a leader of the people you must learn to watch events."

"But what do you mean by watching events?"

"Do you see Mother Carey's stall?" said Dusty, pointing in the direction of the counter of the good-natured widow.

"I should think I did; and what's more, Julia owes her a tick for herrings."

"Right," said Devilsdust, "and nothing but herrings are to be seen on her board. Two years ago it was meat."

"I twig," said Mick.

"Wait till it's wegetables; when the people can't buy even fish. Then we will talk about strikes. That's what I call watching events."'

92 Another prosperous trader recorded by Charles Spurgeon in 1884. The notice claims that W. Thompson, champion pie-maker, has been in business for upwards of fifty years — before this particular salesman was born, in fact. I cannot quite make out the poster in the shop window, except that the Alhambra is advertising a show, possibly a ballet, called *Black Eyed See-usan*.

93　A knife-grinder on Wimbledon Common, 1898. H. Smith, Tinman & Cutler, was in a heavily capitalised business. If he was lucky, he may have inherited the mobile grinding wheel; it would have taken him a good many month's earnings to buy it. He might have hired it; there were plenty of small firms that made more money than the street-traders by hiring out street-traders' equipment; but that would have taken most of the profit out of the tinman's work. In this case the decorative finials above his nameplate suggest that he had a margin in hand for the graces of life. The figures in the background are washerwomen, drying their laundry on lines on Wimbledon Common. Authority would be perturbed if anyone tried to put the common to that use today.

94   The windmill seller: Wimbledon Common, 1898. If you wanted to do well in this line of business you and your wife made the windmills, out of coloured paper and a pin mounted on a wooden stick, and you went out and sold them wherever you could find children with a penny or two to spare. You had to carry the load of windmills on one arm, and run along at a little jog in order to keep the windmill turning on the other. So really you needed to be young and well fed and something of an athlete. If you weren't any of those things—well, you just did the best you could.

95   The window-mender, Greenwich, 1885; one of Charles Spurgeon's studies of London street characters. The picture is sufficient evidence of the precariousness of this particular trade, which depended upon turning up not only when a window needed mending but when its owner happened to be in a position to pay for new glass. The boy half out of the picture on the right is a reminder of the film, *The Kid*, in which Chaplin played an itinerant window-mender and employed a small boy, always one street-corner ahead of him, armed with a suitable supply of stones.

96　The old clothes man, 1885. For a man who could only trade in what he could carry, one might have thought this would be a particularly precarious existence. The old gentleman, however, does not seem to have been doing too badly. His clothes are not torn, his scarf is neatly tied and, perhaps most significant, his shoes have been polished. The particular hazard of this sort of life for an older man was the impossibility of providing for the future. Alan Moore, son of the Norman Moore in Plate 73, wrote of the streets of London in the 1880s: 'Beggars, crossing-sweepers and street musicians abounded. In the background for many lay the workhouse, to be avoided as long as possible but inevitable at last. The poor were badly dressed and dirty, and the smell of a crowd was unpleasant.'

97　The chair mender, Greenwich, 1885. In the days before the telephone, and before do-it-yourself was fashionable, street-traders like this cheerful craftsman were a necessary part of middle-class domestic management. When the leg or the seat of a chair needed mending you did nothing about it at the time; you simply put it on one side until the chair-mender called, which he was sure to do within the next week or two.

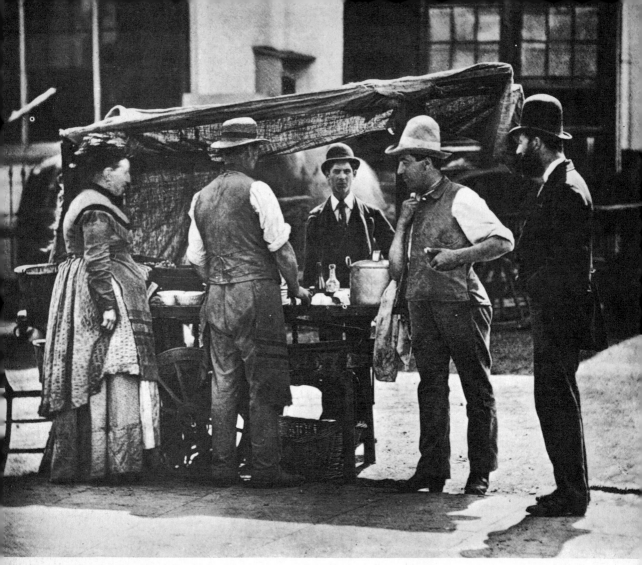

98 A shellfish stall, 1876. Thomson and Smith recorded the proprietor of this stall as saying: 'Find out a prime thirsty spot, which you know by the number of public 'ouses it supports. Oysters, whelks and liquor go together inwariable; consequence where there's fewest stalls and most publics is the choicest spot for a pitch.' The profundity of that truth has changed little in the past hundred years; except, alas, that oysters have long ceased to be a poor man's pleasure.

99 Impulse buying in the 1870s. Thomson and Smith, who took this photograph in about 1876, recorded that dealers in fancy goods, who sold combs and imitation jewellery, were among the most prosperous of all the London stall-holders, perhaps because they did not sell necessities; a woman only bought from them when she was in a mind to be careless about what she spent. The proprietor of this stall remarked: 'Saturday and Monday nights are our best times; when the people are looking through a glass of gin our things seem wonderful tempting, and their little bare-footed youngsters look clothed and warm.'

100 A concert at the street corner; the junction of Weimar Street and Putney High Street in about 1900. In addition to the music from the barrel organ, there is some kind of visual entertainment; possibly a monkey in a cage whose antics can be seen from both sides. But this particular show has been here before, or the children farther down the street would not have been so uninterested.

101 A Boot-black Extraordinary. In an age when the streets of London were frequently muddy and invariably fouled with horse droppings, it is not surprising that there were thousands of boot blacks. Most of them were boys, and in 1877 Thomson and Smith recorded that they were organised in recognised brigades, one brigade of 385 boys earning a total of £12,062. But this bearded and bespectacled boot-black, Jacobus Parker, also recorded by Thomson and Smith, was a very different character. Parker worked for twenty-two years as a vellum binder in the stationery department of the Treasury. At the same time he earned money in the evenings as an actor and dramatic reader. But then he fell ill, lost the sight of an eye, lost his job and finally drifted into Lambeth workhouse. From this plight he was rescued, he claimed, by no less a person than Gladstone, with a gift of £10 which enabled him to set himself up in business cleaning shoes and selling blacking, matches and sweets.

102 and 103   The tough end of the street-trader business; and as usual it is the women who get it. The Putney flower-seller and the Cheapside apple-woman both have their pitches in the road, not on the pavement; presumably this was a police requirement, though it is difficult to see the point of it. The apple-woman must have needed a back and arms of steel; consider the strain of holding a heavy basket of apples in that position for hours at a time.

104   A Whitechapel pub in the 1870s. Thomson and Smith did not record the name of the pub where their picture was taken, but mention that though it was in the centre of the Whitechapel Road, it had not entirely lost its rural character: 'There are still tables and benches placed outside, as if to entice Londoners to sit and enjoy country air, though they are no longer planted on the green sward but on the pavement stone.' The man on the right, with a hook on his left arm, lost the hand in an accident at the Whitechapel coal wharves. Before the accident he had earned a comfortable living as a coal porter, but was having difficulty in providing for himself and his mother when the photograph was taken.

The Pub

In an age when drink was a much more serious social problem than it is now, many of London's pubs were little more than places where a man could spend such money as he had on anaesthesia or oblivion. But some managed to retain the qualities of the village inn. Our Victorian ancestors seem to have been rather fonder than we are of taking their drink sitting out-of-doors, and pubs in suburban London owed much of their summer trade to the possession of a tea-garden, even though tea may not have been the liquor consumed. Others owed their popularity to being on a river, or near enough to the country to give their patrons the feeling that they had momentarily escaped from the city. This aspect of pub-going satisfied the kind of urge that Londoners now feel when they get into their cars to escape from London on a fine evening or during the weekend.

105   The Black Lion in
Church Street, Chelsea, in the
1860s. Mr J. E. Hudson, the
landlord, whose placards
proclaim that he is a wine
and spirit merchant as well
as being Truman, Hanbury,
Buxton & Comps. Entire,
devoted his largest capital letters to his Tea Gardens. The
garden may have been no
more than the space between
the wooden fence and the
whitewashed wall, but it was
evidently a draw to custom.

106   The Leather Bottle in Garratt Lane between Wandsworth and Tooting, about 1880. The
Leather Bottle still stands, though inevitably it has lost the air of almost rural calm that characterised
it ninety years ago. Three of the customers are enjoying their drinks on the bench outside. Possibly they
are the owners of the bread tricycle and the barrel organ, and are keeping an eye on their property.

107 The Feathers Boat House on the Wandle at Wandsworth. The clothes suggest the late 1860s or early '70s. The Feathers was, of course, a pub as well as a boat house, as is clear from the notices over the door: 'Young and Bainbridges Entire.' In the past hundred years the pleasant Wandle, as it was when the photograph was taken, has joined the sad company of London's decayed little rivers, opaque with industrial effluent, that contribute to the fouling of the Thames.

108 The garden of the Bowyer Arms, Manor Street, Clapham, in 1909. A garden was a great asset for the licensee, not only for the enjoyment of his own family but because it attracted custom during the summer months. This garden is well cared for, but notice the roughness of the grass. Sixty years ago the precision-mowing of lawns was a lot less important than it is now.

109 and 110 The Bull's Head at Barnes and the White Hart at Mortlake, both photographed by E. P. Olney in 1912. Though these public houses have been modernised, the Thames, at least at Barnes, is not greatly changed. What has changed, and alas has probably vanished for ever, is the atmosphere of unhurried peace and tranquility that went out with the last days of horse transport. To the left of the coffee room of the White Hart is a stationary traction engine which I find difficult to account for. It looks considerably older than the date of the photograph, 1912, but that is not strange, because such engines are noted for their longevity. But what is it doing? The flywheel is turning (the spokes are invisible), so perhaps the engine is being used for road repairs or other works connected with the small pile of rubble lying by it.

111   The Spaniards, Hampstead, in the golden age. The surface of the road indicates the passage of carts, carriages and bicycles — but not yet of motor cars. The photograph was probably taken around 1900, and the scene had changed little if at all since Dickens's day, when it was recorded that Mrs Bardell's party 'walked forth, in quest of a Hampstead stage. This was soon found, and in a couple of hours they all arrived safely in the Spaniards Tea-gardens.' It was on this occasion that Mrs Raddle made the extravagant error of ordering tea for seven, when, as all the ladies agreed, young Tommy Bardell could perfectly well have drunk out of someone else's cup when the waiter wasn't looking, thereby saving the price of one tea. Mrs Bardell and her party would still recognise the scene today; though of course they could not stand in the road, at the point from which the photograph was taken, without being instantly knocked down. It must be regarded as little short of a miracle that the bottleneck formed by the inn and the toll-house have, as I write, still escaped the destructive instincts of the road-planners.

Time Off

In the middle years of the nineteenth century, London's working classes enjoyed few holidays. As in so many other aspects of life, they were worse off than either their grandfathers or their grandsons. They were caught midway between the 'holy-days' of former centuries and the concept, new in an industrial society, of a week or a fortnight given as a holiday with pay. The sharply diminishing number of saints-day holidays is shown by the records of the Bank of England: in 1761 the Bank closed on 47 saints-days, in 1808 on 44 and in 1825 on 40; but by 1834 there were only four such days, which has remained the English practice ever since. On the other hand, granting of holidays with pay as a part of the terms of employment did not become widespread until the 1890s and later. Apart from Sundays, therefore, the only time off was Saturday afternoon, and even that was not universal. For shop assistants one half-day off a week, other than Sunday, did not become statutory until the Shops Act of 1911. Under such circumstances it is hardly surprising that leisure activities, as we understand them, did not flourish in London except among those who were comparatively rich. Only a few traditions, such as the annual saturnalia of Derby Day and the paid holiday of hop-picking, served to keep alive what was left of the holiday gaiety that had characterised Londoners in earlier centuries.

112   Derby Day: the Clapham Road in the 1890s. A contemporary account in *Round London* describes the scene in the Clapham Road on the morning of Derby Day as being 'animated in the extreme. The genteel folk that inhabit the villas survey the amazing and seemingly endless procession of equipages, which range from a lordly four-in-hand to a coster's donkey-barrow, from the seclusion of their own front rooms.'

113 Donkey rides on Clapham Common in the 1870s. According to Thomson and Smith the owners of these donkeys did best on Sundays and Good Fridays. The cost of keeping a donkey was reckoned to be 1*s*. 6*d*. a day; and by giving rides on the Common the owner could reckon to take about 10*s*. during the day, and even as much as £1 or 30*s*. on Good Fridays.

114 Swearing on the Horn, Highgate: March 1906. Considering the size of London, and the number of villages that the capital has swallowed up, surprisingly few traditions of this kind survived through the nineteenth century. Even this example has the air of a self-conscious revival. An early account of the ceremony reads: 'Most of the public houses in Highgate have a large pair of horns placed over the sign; when the country people stop for refreshment a pair of large horns, fixed to the end of a staff, is brought to them, and they are earnestly pressed to be sworn. If they consent, a kind of burlesque oath is administered that they will never eat brown bread when they can get white, never kiss the maid when they can kiss the mistress, and abundance of other things of the same kind.'

115   A Fairlop Boat at Barkingside, Ilford, in 1900. I am indebted to Mr Hellicar and Mr Herbert
Ward of the Bancroft Road Public Library for the following information about the Fairlop Boat
tradition: 'The Fairlop Boat custom originated in the 1700s, when Daniel Day, a master pump- and
block-maker of Wapping, used to take his workmen to his house near Hainault Forest by a boat on
wheels, and there to entertain them to dinner. The event was held on the first Friday in July under the
branches of an ancient tree known as the Fairlop oak, and in time it developed into a fair—the
Fairlop Fair. After Hainault Forest was disafforested, revellers went instead to a field opposite the
Old Maypole Inn, Barkingside, and later to the Bald Hind at Chigwell. Other boats were built, and
the custom spread from Wapping to Poplar. Boats were laid up during the year and brought out only
on "Fairlop Friday". The fair was last held, it seems, in a meadow behind the Old Maypole in about
1899, but it is believed that one or another of the boats were used for outings until early in the
present century. What is said to have been the last boat built, in 1890, was bought in 1910 and set up
in a garden in Romford.'

95

116 Picking flowers on Wimbledon Common, 1881. Those who know the Common today will observe the effect of generations of flower-pickers; the wild flowers have virtually disappeared. The photograph is a sad reminder that townsmen, if they visit the surrounding country in large numbers, invariably destroy the pleasures that they set out to enjoy.

117 and 118 Quoits in a Highgate garden, 1895. These charmingly ingenuous attempts at action pictures sprang from the necessity of holding a pose for long enough to meet the needs of the camera of the day. The pose taken up by the bearded gentleman in the white flannel suit suggests that in the back of his mind he has a vague recollection of Myron's *Discobolus*—reasonably enough, because the game of quoits is said to be descended from the sport of throwing the discus. Quoits still survives, of course; for those who do not know the game, it consists of throwing metal rings a distance of 18 yards into a bed of wet clay in which stands a small pin or hob. Points are scored by getting the quoit over the peg or as close to it as possible.

119   Hop-picking: the traditional Cockney holiday. Though this is
not a London photograph, I felt justified in including it in a book
about London because hop-picking became such a deeply engrained
habit among East End Londoners. It only began to die out with the
introduction of hop-picking machinery in the 1960s, long after
holidays with pay and a rising standard of living had made it econ-
omically outdated. It is easy to tell the visiting pickers from the
locals by distinguishing those who are dressed for work from those
who are dressed to kill. Notice the umbrella on the hop-pole; suntan
was to be avoided at all costs.

The Bicycle

The coming of the bicycle gave to London's man-in-the-street the same sense of liberation that the railways had brought to the average villager. Both provided those of modest means with a sense of mobility and therefore of freedom. The penny-farthing in the 1870s, and the pneumatic-tyred free-wheeling safety-bicycle in the 1880s and later, enabled wage-earners to escape from London into the country on Sundays, just as the mass-produced motor-car does today. But the bicycle had one great advantage over the car; it was able to use the existing country roads, and the highways left over from the great days of coaching. It did not pollute the air with noise and fumes, and it did not destroy the character of the country towns and villages through which it passed.

The golden pen of Richard Church, writing of his childhood in South London in *Over the Bridge*, paints an unforgettable picture of the sense of escape that bicycling brought to his own family in the early years of this century. 'As we drew out of the inner suburbs towards Kingston the clouds broke and the rain ceased. We stopped on the Portsmouth Road to discard our dry macintoshes and to eat some raisins. But excitement would have carried us on without the help of other nourishment. This was my first great journey by road. . . .

'The traffic thinned out, the suburbs dropped away (for London was smaller 50 years ago), the countryside grew deeper, wider, more lush. We crossed the Surrey commons, and for the first time in my life I heard larks trilling in the sky. . . .

'The roads were plain macadam, an inch deep in dust of many colours, the tints varying with the nature of the road metal used by the local councils. But the over-all hue was cement-grey; a fine, choking powder that gradually settled along the creases of our skin, our garments, and on every plain surface. By the time we reached Guildford we were three millers . . . During the fierce afternoon, to the wonder of the townsfolk and villagers we trundled along through Farnham and Alton, past lovely parks, pine woods, farmsteads, over streams and round hillsides, further and further from London, and from our familiar selves, the world growing stranger and wilder, and we with it, until at last, as dusk fell, we stumbled off our machines in the tiny lane before the meadow-fronted cottages, fabulous beings no longer in command of our limbs, or our wits.'

120   Where the city man's bicycling dreams began. Riding a penny-farthing was difficult; it was not just something you could pick up by watching others. The point of this photograph, taken in Aldgate in the 1870s, is the advertisement for the City Bicycle School in Chequer Yard. The illustration in the oval, which I can just make out with a magnifying glass, shows a dashing young man on a penny-farthing sailing loftily past an admiring young woman. Today's driving schools have longer pedigrees than we realise.

121   Prepare to mount.... One of the attractions of old photographs is the information that they provide on techniques of which no written record remains, simply because no one bothered to write it down. Here is precise evidence on the correct procedure for mounting a penny-farthing. You had, of course, to push off with your right foot, as though on a scooter, until the bicycle was moving fast enough to enable you to keep it balanced while you got into the saddle. It was a long way to fall if you made a mistake. Some models had no brakes; the substitute was back-pressure on the pedals.

122   A London bicycling club on its way through the suburbs on a winter morning. Bicycling in the 1870s was smart, dashing and manly, and it was much less expensive than keeping a horse. This club wear a uniform of cap, jacket, breeches and dark stockings, though their machines include a variety of penny-farthing bicycles and different patterns of tricycles. The additional weight of the tricycle must have counted against its greater safety and convenience, though, to judge from this picture, there was no feeling at the time that riding the safer alternative was unmanly.

123　A tricycle made for
two — less efficient but a great
deal more sociable than the
later tandem safety-bicycle
that Daisy Bell was assured
she would look sweet on the
seat of. Riding a penny-
farthing bicycle would have
been totally unfeminine, but a
tricycle of this kind could be
ridden discreetly in a skirt.

124　Sir Henry Kimber and a party of tricyclists during a run in the 1880s. He appears to be giving
instructions regarding their route, possibly from a map in his hand. Though the uniform is laxer than
in Plate 122, three of the members in this group are wearing a Maltese cross in their headgear. The
tricycles show an important technical advance on those in the preceding pictures: two of them have
the chain-and-pedal propulsion that was the essential characteristic of the safety-bicycle.

125 Penny-farthings and tricycles at the New Inn, Ham Common. The riders may have called for a drink on their way down the Portsmouth Road; more probably Ham Common was the objective of a shorter run out of London. Clearly they are members of a club, wearing peaked caps and cap badges, and more or less the same uniform of jacket, breeches and stockings. If any of them went back today they would recognise the New Inn corner immediately, but they would find the road from Ham to Richmond, running out of the picture on the right, somewhat less pleasant for bicycling, and distinctly more dangerous. In this picture, as in Plate 122, there is no suggestion that the safer and easier tricycle was less becoming to young manhood than the pennyfarthing; this group shows three of each. Even today Ham, though swallowed up by the growth of outer London, retains much of its country atmosphere; but when these lucky cyclists pedalled out on a Sunday morning they really were in the country.

Carriages and Cabs

Keeping a private carriage in Victorian and Edwardian London was much more of a luxury than keeping a car is today. The term 'carriage-folk' was used with respect and almost with awe of those who could afford such expenditure. In this matter life in London was very different from life in the country. A man who had only two or three acres of grass could keep his own pony, and drive it to a gig, at little cost. But the man who kept a horse in London had to pay not only for the stable but for hay and oats all the year round, winter and summer, whether the horse was being used or standing idle. Moreover, a horse in a stable required constant grooming and cleaning-out, and this entailed paying wages and finding board and lodging for a groom. Families who could not afford their own groom, or who had no stabling of their own, could solve that part of the problem by keeping their horses at the nearest livery stable, of which there was one in every good residential district. London's middle classes, however, used their feet a great deal more than we do. Trollope's elderly Q.C., Mr Abel Wharton, was rich enough to live in the expensive Manchester Square, but even he used public transport, and walked home from his chambers in the Temple every day.

126   Marshall's Livery and Bait Stables in Putney, about 1903. This was the equivalent in its day of the local garage and service station. Mr Marshall's shop-front proclaims that he is a Job Master, that is to say he offers horses and carriages to let on hire for either riding or driving. For the family who only needed a carriage once or twice a week this was much the most economical system. 'Livery stables' meant that Mr Marshall would make a contract to keep a customer's own horse, and possibly carriage, for an agreed charge by the week, month or year. 'Bait stables' meant that a customer who wanted to shop or pay a business call in the neighbourhood could leave his horse with Mr Marshall for the hour or the day; the horse would be fed and watered as required. A bait stable was in effect the equivalent of a multi-storey car park, but relatively more expensive.

127 A dog-cart in a south London suburb. This is a neat little turn-out with an attractive pony, but it would not have been thought particularly stylish in its day. The mudguards, though no doubt practical, were for some reason considered to detract from the smartness of a carriage of this kind.

128 A pony-chaise at Granville Road, Southfields. This is a more expensive and stylish turn-out than the dog-cart in plate 127. Both are driven by women, and in each case there is no protection from the weather, other than the rug over the knees.

129 A City man in his Lawton gig in the year 1900. Both the gig and the horse are typical of the carriages used for driving daily between the owner's home and office. The groom would travel as a passenger to the City, take the gig home and bring it back at the end of the working day. It was considered much smarter for a man to drive his own gig well than to be driven.

105

130   Four-wheel cabs or 'growlers' outside a South Eastern Railway station in Greenwich, in 1885. Growlers were the equivalent of taxis in their day and had a roof-rack for luggage. They were licensed to carry a maximum of five passengers, and the fares were laid down by regulation, just as taxi fares are now. In 1876 the fare was 6*d.* for a mile or part of a mile, and 2*s.* for an hour or part of an hour. For every 15 minutes or part of 15 minutes above one hour, a quarter of the hourly rate was charged. Waiting-time was charged at a quarter of the hourly rate for each 15 minutes. No fare could be less than 1*s.* For each passenger beyond two there was a supplementary charge of 6*d.*; 2*d.* was charged for every item of luggage carried on the roof. Note that these rates were expensive compared with today's taxi fares. A shilling then was a good deal more than 10*s.* is now.

131   A Thomas Tilling hansom cab, 1885. The hansom cab was often spoken of in its day as the gondola of London. It would carry two passengers, as well as luggage on the roof, and was successful because it was light, quick and handy. Passengers could talk to the driver through a trap-door in the roof, though the door could be closed by courting couples who wanted privacy. Note that the boy in this photograph is not a genuine passenger—he has presumably got in to oblige the photographer. No self-respecting driver would have driven off with the shafts up in the air and his cab so hopelessly out of balance. It was part of the driver's art to trim his cab and make the load as easy as possible for his horse. With two fat passengers the shafts would come down smartly, and the driver would throw his weight backwards to ease the load on the horse's back. With one light passenger he would have thrown his weight forward. Tillings were a big firm with a great reputation in the streets of London, running a fleet of buses as well as hansom cabs.

132 A Thomas Tilling omnibus on the Putney–Clapham route. Inside passengers enjoyed protection from the weather; those on top made the best of rugs and umbrellas. Unoccupied seats on top were protected with a canvas cover, which the conductor fastened over when it was raining; new passengers were thus spared the discomfort of sitting down in a pool of water. The value of advertising space, both inside and outside buses, was appreciated from the early days.

Public Transport

During the second half of the nineteenth century London developed a system of buses, trams and trains that became the envy of the civilised world. Even today's buses and underground trains have an ancestry that goes back for a century or more; the buses are recognisable descendants of those of the 1870s, and the District and Inner Circle railways run on tracks and through stations that our great-grandfathers would still find familiar. Although today's buses are capable of speeds much greater than those of the horse buses, actual journey times are hardly any faster because of the congested traffic. Some years ago, in a BBC programme, I introduced a bus driver, then an old man, who had started work on horse-drawn buses and was still driving in 1947. He assured me that a journey from Hampstead to St Paul's took no longer in the horse days than it did in the late 1940s.

133   The view from the top of a horse-drawn bus.
The top of a bus was recognised as the best
grandstand for seeing the sights of London, and was
used for that purpose by all classes. These young
women, on Ludgate Hill in 1897, are almost
certainly using the bus to admire the decorations
for Queen Victoria's Diamond Jubilee.

134 A knifeboard bus at the foot of Rosslyn Hill, Hampstead, in June 1887. It ran on the route to Tottenham Court Road, Oxford Street and Piccadilly Circus; a notice across the corner of the coachwork reads: 'near Euston Station'. The third horse was used to help pull the load up the hill. At the top of the hill it was unhitched and taken down to the bottom, ready for the next bus. Some horses became so familiar with this job that they were left to find their own way down and wait unattended at the bottom. They were known as trace-horses or cock-horses, though it is doubtful whether many of today's parents or children, who go through the traditional motions of the nursery-rhyme, realise what the latter term means.

135 A London General Omnibus Company bus on the run from Tottenham to Millwall Dock. The photograph was taken in 1913, shortly after this service was introduced. The design of the bus has changed very little, compared with the preceding three pictures, except that someone has taken the horses away and put an engine in their place. Guard rails have been added between front and back wheels, in an attempt to protect pedestrians.

136   A horse-drawn tram on the route from
Greenwich to Westminster, via Deptford, New
Cross and the Old Kent Road, in 1885. Trams first
appeared on the streets of London in the 1860s, but
there was considerable opposition to them because
it was claimed that the rails were a hazard to other
traffic. The efficiency of the tram compared with the
omnibus can be seen by comparing the passenger
accommodation of this vehicle with that in Plates
132 and 134.

110

137 One of London's first electric trams, on
Brixton Hill in the 1890s. The similarity in design
between the horse-drawn and electric tram is even
more striking than between the horse bus and the
early motor-bus. The electric current was picked up
from a slotted middle rail. Notice the sign-board
above the letters LCC, proclaiming that this is a
workmen's car — that is to say, a special cheap
service. Fares were 'all the way 1*d*., return 2*d*.,
ordinary $\frac{1}{2}d$. fares'. Those were the days.

111

138 Cold comfort for commuters. A third-class compartment, with hard wooden seats, at Lewisham Junction in 1885. The picture provides a useful exercise for those who complain too loudly of discomfort on Southern Region suburban trains in the 1970s. These 1885 trains were not heated; and passengers who wanted to read after dark provided their own light in the form of candle-lanterns, which they carried to work with them.

139 Victoria Station in the great days of steam. Here is another picture that may help to dispel the illusion that the railways in the good old days were better run than they are today. Every train under the glass roof dispensed its quota of smoke and grime, most of which stayed there because there was nowhere else for it to go. Mrs Richard Moore has kindly sent me the following note from her family's correspondence: 'The underground railway had not long been opened (1869). From then until the twentieth century the trains were drawn by steam. Everything was covered with soot. To open a carriage door blackened your hand. After a train had left the station the opposite platform was hardly visible for smoke. The smoke had a peculiarly strong smell and used to billow up through gratings in the streets.'

The Traffic Problem

Traffic congestion has been a problem in cities since cities began. The Ancient Romans were always complaining of it. But there is no doubt that in Victorian London the streets were safer than they are today, in the sense that pedestrians were less likely to be knocked down if they crossed the road without looking where they were going. There were of course no petrol fumes, but there were plenty of disagreeable smells of other kinds. And the noise must have been tremendous. To quote again from the Moore family records, for the year 1869: 'London was grimy and very noisy. Most of the City streets were paved with granite setts, and on them the waggons with iron-tyred wheels made a din that prevented conversation while they passed by. All the various carts and private carriages, landaus, victorias and broughams had iron tyres. The roar of London by day was almost terrible—a never-varying deep rumble that made a background to all other sounds.'

140   Hyde Park Corner from St George's Hospital, 1903. The buses in the foreground are of the kind complained of by the medical student in the caption to Plate 75. Most of the vehicles on the far side of the road are hansom cabs and growlers, but two smart open carriages are making their way northward into Hyde Park. Notice the self-confident stride of the top-hatted figure in the foreground.

141 Looking east along Oxford Street from Oxford Circus, with Peter Robinson's on the left. The carriage on the left, drawn by two horses, is a landau with its leather hoods closed. With the hoods down it would become a completely open carriage. Notice that several pedestrians are walking in the road in front of it, without even a glance at it. Presumably today's jay-walking is a hereditary disease.

142 Trafalgar Square and St Martin's-in-the-
Fields in 1902. If it is studied with a magnifying
glass this will be seen to be another splendid
example of pedestrians wandering all over the road
without paying the slightest attention to the traffic.
Bicycling must have been a very agreeable way of
getting about London at the turn of the
century.

143　Wandsworth High Street, looking towards
the parish church. At first sight this seems to be an
example of one-way traffic. In fact, it is not, or is
not meant to be; near the church two vehicles are
moving away from the camera. The rest are merely
a case of the Londoner's disregard for lane-
discipline, then as now.

144 The dinner hour. The standard practice among carters and van drivers was to let a horse drink from the nearest water-trough when he needed to, and to carry his feed in a nosebag. The horse was often left to feed unattended while the driver slipped off to get a little something for himself. The photograph is a reminder of the granite setts with which so many London streets were paved, and which contributed largely to the noise of the traffic.

145 and 146   A London filling-station at the turn
of the century. The familiar contemporary problem
of the motorist in London—where to find
somewhere to get a fill—was easier to solve in the
days of horses. Troughs like this one were provided
all over the capital by the Metropolitan Drinking
Fountain and Cattle Trough Association, and
indeed some of them still survive. Plate 146 shows
in one picture both types of London cab: the
hansom (*left*) and the slower four-wheeled growler.

118

Public Services

In the public services of a city as large as London there would be ample material for a whole book of photographs; no attempt is made in this section to deal with them thoroughly, and indeed the greater part have necessarily been left out. The fire brigade photographs are, however, a reminder of how completely the safety of London depended, almost until the end of the nineteenth century, on the muscle and speed of horses. The Royal Mail, born and bred in the days of horse transport and directly descended from the Roman mail service in this respect, took to mechanisation at the earliest possible moment, and made use of the bicycle from the days of the penny-farthing. But even when the post depended on the combination of steam on the railways and horses on the road, Londoners were provided with a better service than we get today. In 1876 evening mails from London to the country left at 8 p.m., and letters in normal pillar-boxes had to be posted before 5.30 p.m.; there was a late acceptance until 7.45 p.m. on payment of a fee of 1s. at the portico of the G.P.O. in St Martin's-le-Grand. Within London itself, however, there were actually twelve deliveries daily. The following is taken from Post Office regulations published in a desk diary of 1876. 'The first or general despatch is made from St Martin's-le-Grand at about 7.30 a.m., and the delivery is generally completed throughout London by 9 o'clock, except on Mondays or when there are large arrivals of letters from abroad. The last despatch is made at 7.45 p.m. All letters for these deliveries should bear the district initials to prevent delay.' Postage rates on inland letters were 1d. for an ounce, $1\frac{1}{2}d.$ for two ounces and so on up to 4d. for 12 ounces. The advantage of twelve postal deliveries a day in a commercial and financial city like London was, of course, much more significant before the coming of the telephone.

147　The public disinfection service in London in the 1870s. Thomson and Smith in *Street Life in London*, published in 1877, remarked rather sanctimoniously: 'Our recent sanitary legislation has called into existence a class of men who must of necessity be daily exposed to the gravest dangers — the public disinfectors. These modest heroes are truly typical of our advanced civilisation.' When a case of smallpox or other infectious disease was notified to the authorities the disinfectors called at the house with their hand-cart. 'Once in the sick-room,' recorded Thomson and Smith, 'they have strict orders to exclude everyone from their dangerous presence. Alone and unseen they remove, one by one, all the clothes, bedding, carpets, curtains, in fact all textile materials they can find in the room, carefully place them in the cart, and drag them off to the disinfecting-oven. This is, of course, a dangerous operation, as the dust it occasions must be loaded with the zymotic particles that engender epidemics. Few persons care to be present on these occasions; and, but for their own honesty of purpose, the disinfectors might often make away with various objects which in all probability would not at first be missed.'

148 Kensington Fire Brigade in about 1890. Though horses were required to pull the engine to the fire, the pumping engine itself was steam-driven. Those with an eye for a horse will notice what a fine pair these are and how well they are turned-out. The horses used by the London fire brigades were celebrated as being among the best draught horses to be found.

149 Kensington Vestry fire service in 1862. As the term Vestry indicates, local government services were still organised in London on a parish basis. The disinfector's cart in Plate 147 was also organised on a Vestry basis, as was the collection of refuse; in fact, the term for a dust cart during the 19th century was a Vestry cart.

150　An L.C.C. self-propelled fire engine of 1909.
This must have represented a major technical
advance in its day, though one can imagine the kind
of rear-guard action that would have been fought by
the champions of the horse—claiming, probably
with justification, that their horse-drawn fire
engines would be harnessed and away long before
this contraption could be started up.

151 A London postman of 1885. The photograph was taken nine years after the publication of the Post Office regulations quoted on page 120, but the penny post was still in force and, indeed, one of the pillars of the national economy. It was not finally overtaken by inflation until 1918, and even then remained valid for postcards, with letters at $1\frac{1}{2}d.$, until 1940, exactly a century after it was introduced.

152 A tricycle-mounted postman of 1903. The quarters of the horse, in the Royal Mail van just visible behind him, are a reminder that mail vans, like fire engines, were noted for the quality of the horses that drew them, though they did not require the same turn of speed.

153   The march of progress: a G.P.O. Maudslay van of 1911. The mails were given distinctly better protection from the weather than the driver and his mate, though the hood on the rudimentary cab could be lowered when it rained. Private cars of the day were already fitted with glass windscreens, but that appears to have been considered an unnecessary luxury by the G.P.O.

125

Journey's End

154 and 155   The funeral of a London shopkeeper. This is not, as one might suppose, the cortège of an elder statesman, about to be laid to his rest in Westminster Abbey, but that of quite a modest London retailer. Never in his life would he have enjoyed anything approaching this awesome display of affluence and respect; but for some reason it was considered, in the year 1901, that at his death nothing less would do. We owe the survival of this record to Sir Benjamin Stone, who, almost alone among his contemporaries, realised that such pictures would be of interest to future generations. He sent the photographs to his friend Dr Dan McKenzie, of Leytonstone, just after he had taken them. Dr McKenzie replied, on December 5th, 1901, 'The pictures you have been able to secure will, I am sure, be of interest to future historians of the morals and manners of the nineteenth century. Two more thorough specimens of the mourners of the world you could not hope to find than in these dreadful mutes...'

Perhaps the two mutes were themselves vaguely conscious that at this funeral, in December 1901, they were mourning not only the death of a local shopkeeper but the end of the Victorian era, and the final conclusion of a long and august episode in English history.

Index